The
Garland Library
of
War and Peace

The
Garland Library
of
War and Peace

Under the General Editorship of

Blanche Wiesen Cook, *John Jay College, C.U.N.Y.*

Sandi E. Cooper, *Richmond College, C.U.N.Y.*

Charles Chatfield, *Wittenberg University*

The Universal Peace Organization of King George of Bohemia

A Fifteenth Century Plan for World Peace
1462/1464

by

Jiři z Poděbrad

translated from the original Latin
by
Members of the Czechoslovak Academy

with a new introduction
for the Garland Edition by
F. G. Heymann

Garland Publishing, Inc., New York & London
1972

Library of Congress Cataloging in Publication Data

Jiří z Poděbrad, King of Bohemia, 1420-1471.
    The universal peace organization of King George of
Bohemia.

    (The Garland library of war and peace)
    Includes bibliographical references.
    CONTENTS: Historical significance of the peace
project of King George of Bohemia and the research
problems involved, by V. Vaněček.--Tractatus pacis toti
christianitati fiendae, edidit, J. Kejř.--Editorial
note. [etc.]
    1. International organization--History. 2. Peace.
I. Title. II. Series.

JX1942.J513 1972   341'.172   78-147413
ISBN 0-8240-0211-3

Printed in the United States of America

Introduction

At a certain point in the later middle ages, it became increasingly obvious that the dream of Christian unity, dominated by a Roman emperor and a Roman pope, had been shattered. Pope and emperor fought each other more frequently than they collaborated. The French kings, once staunch defenders of the papacy in its struggle with the Hohenstaufens, strengthened their position in relation to Rome and gained a special importance during the "Babylonian Captivity" at Avignon which ended in the Great Schism. The conciliar movements which followed appeared to reduce absolutist papal power for a time, but by the conclusion of the Council of Basel, the new authority of the councils was eroded. Enea Silvio de' Piccolomini had sided with the conciliar position in his earlier years; as cardinal and finally as Pope Pius II, he embraced the view that unlimited papal power was essential to the maintenance of Catholic Christianity. His general policy, the elimination of all challenges to the papacy, was epitomized in the bull, Execrabilis (1460).[1]

Europe, particularly its eastern regions, was gravely menaced by Turkish expansion in the fifteenth and

[1] *See the* Commentaries of Pius II (Smith College Studies in History, *vol. XXV, Book III), p. 276 f.*

early sixteenth centuries. The papacy and the Curia were more conscious of the dangers than most other rulers and leaders. Pope Pius failed in his attempts to mount a Christian resistance. The long tradition of warfare, between French and English, between Poles and Teutonic Knights, between Hungarians and Venetians, among the princes of the Holy Roman Empire — to note a few cases — nullified efforts at a unified front. In the fourteenth and fifteenth centuries, several rulers and Holy Roman emperors had tried to limit or eliminate the continuous warfare with little success. The erosion of imperial authority, particularly under the Hapsburgs Albert II (1438-39) and Frederick III (1440-1493), made their efforts futile exercises. Nonetheless, the longing continued for some reasonable organization and cooperation among the political bodies of Europe.

In this background of strained relations between papacy and secular rulers, and the background of seemingly endless warfare among princes, and the looming Turkish threat, there developed the religious crisis engendered by the appearance of Hussitism in central Europe. After a long war (1419-1436) the Council of Basel accepted the Compacts of the Hussite movement and recognized the right of the laity to use the chalice. The Hussite-Utraquist Church was thus born and continued to exist for a time.[2]

[2] *For the Compacts, see R. Urbánek*, Věk poděbradský *(České dějiny, III, 1) vol. 1 (Prague, 1915), pp. 88-136. For an English treatment, see F. Heymann*, George of Bohemia, King of Heretics *(Princeton, 1965), pp. 6-12, 38-40, etc.*

6

INTRODUCTION

This religious reformation, prefiguring the Great Reformation of the following century touched off by Martin Luther, was rooted mainly in Bohemia and Moravia, and exercised only tangential influence in Central Europe. It survived the bitter political battles of the imperial interregnum during the mid-fifteenth century. With the rise of Lord George of Poděbrady to eminence in Prague in 1448, the new Church acquired a firm defender. In 1452 the Czech Diet elected George to rule as regent during the minority of King Albert II's posthumously born child, Ladislav.[3] With the unexpected death of the boy-king in 1457, George was elected king by the Czech Diet.[4] He had worked tirelessly as regent to effect a reorganization of the kingdom. Since the early fourteenth century, he was the first — and last — true Czech to become king and ruler. As the "Hussite King" he fought and maintained the freedom of the Utraquist Church.

For a brief time, it appeared as if the papacy would accept George as king. He and Pius II had met once, before either had attained prominence. In 1455, Aeneas Silvius[5] recommended to Pope Calixtus III that the Compacts, if accepted, would bring the more cautious Utraquists nearer to the Catholic world. But

[3] *Heymann, op. cit., pp. 81-95.*

[4] *See Otakar Odlozilik,* The Hussite King *(New Brunswick, 1965), pp. 89-99, and R. Urbánek,* O volbě Jiřího z Poděbrad za Krále českého *(Prague, 1958).*

[5] *See Howard Kaminsky, "Pius Aeneas among the Taborites,"* Church History, *XXVIII (September, 1959), 281-309.*

7

INTRODUCTION

the same man, now pope, expected that the king, confirmed in his election by Rome, would return his people to the strict Ecclesia Catholica, *and would, with the Compacts, even end the use of the chalice by the laity. George knew full well that any attempt to eradicate the Hussite church — ably led by the reformer John Rokycana[6] — would lead to civil and religious war. For years the majority of the reformed religious community and the important Catholic minority had lived in peace. None wanted to return to the torture of the days of the long wars.*

King George's pacific policies gained recognition outside Bohemia. At his death, the great Polish clergyman and historian, Jan Dlugosz wrote "this King had never liked to use the blood of his people." [7] The Czech king's relations with the emperor, Frederick III, and with numerous of the princes and dukes within the Holy Roman Empire, was characterized by patient negotiation and peaceful policies. His influence had even succeeded in reducing the frequent outbursts of war among the petty rulers in the Empire.

Unfortunately, the Czech ruler had far less success with the Roman Church. In 1462 the Pope told a Czech delegation that "he revoked and annihilated the Compacts granted by the Council of Basel to the Bohemians" and that "he has put under ban (and

[6] *See F. Heymann, "John Rokycana — Church Reformer between Hus and Luther,"* Church History, *XXVIII (1959), 240-280.*

[7] *See T. Dlugosz, quoted in Odlozilík, op. cit., p. 264 and p. 305, n.581.*

8

INTRODUCTION

strictly forbidden) the communion in two kinds to the lay people. . . ." [8] *One of the delegates in the negotiations had written*

> *By the goodness of God and the wise, circumspect leadership of King George, all those sufferings and storms have finally ceased and such blessed peace has returned as not the oldest people of the kingdom and the margraviate (Moravia) can remember. This peace the King has brought not only to his own lands, but he has worked to spread it even to the lands of neighbouring kings, princes and lords, as he knows that where there is strife and hatred there is also instability and misery; but where there is peace and concord there also the land is blessed with every happiness.*

The king reacted sharply to the papal condemnation. When a papal legate, sent by Pius II to Prague, threatened the king before the Diet with excommunication and deposition if he did not accept the pope's pronouncement, King George had him imprisoned for several weeks. Perhaps this was impolitic, for it angered strict Catholics. [9] *Nevertheless, King George managed to preserve domestic peace at least to the spring of 1467. At that point, a coalition of barons who claimed they were defending Catholicism began to mount political attacks. It was clear they wanted to regain their previous position of power in the State and unseat the brilliant ruler.* [10]

[8] *See Heymann,* George of Bohemia, *pp. 262-278.*

[9] Ibid., *pp. 281-288 and Odlozilík,* The Hussite King, *pp. 135-140.*

[10] *See Heymann, op. cit., pp. 387 ff.*

9

INTRODUCTION

George intended to fight his deposition and then maintain himself as the head of a lay state independent of Rome. As regent and king, his reforms had produced a healthy legal system and a prospering economy — factors important both to Catholics and Utraquists. Among his servants he was careful to include Catholics as well as Hussites. Having taken an oath to the King, these men refused to accede to the demands from Rome.[11] Support was forthcoming from important friends in the Empire as well, such as the dukes of Saxony and the Margrave (later Elector) Albert Achilles of Brandenburg. The result was that an astonishing number of Catholic lords and knights stood with the king.

Outside the Empire the most consistent and loyal support came from Casimir IV of Poland who also had been a papal candidate for the Czech throne. Though a member of the Polish Jagellion dynasty did mount the throne after George's death, Casimir did not dare attempt any such takeover in the 1460's. Responding to papal pressure, he wrote "I would not want to believe that an anointed and crowned King could be deposed." (1467)[12] Casimir and George developed fairly close ties. Already in 1462 they had met at Glogów (Silesia) where they declared a mutual assistance agreement in the event of Turkish attacks.

[11] *See, e.g., the latter* Dialogus *written by Jan of Rabstejn, ed. by B. Ryba (Prague, 1946).*

[12] *See J.J. Müller,* Des Heiligen Römischen Reiches Reichstags-Theatrum *(Jena, 1713) II, 266.*

10

INTRODUCTION

Further, George authorized the use of Czech mercenaries by Poland in its struggle against the Teutonic Knights (1454-1466). This remarkable relationship is documented in Polish and Czech sources as well as in the historical material contained in The Universal Peace Organization.

Casimir became the first supporter of George's remarkable peace plan, outside of Bohemia. Together these two rulers were to associate themselves and take the first steps toward the practical implementation of the project.

The project, of course, was not the work of the Czech king alone. In its planning stages, important contributions were made by the French-Italian, Antoine Marini, a trusted advisor of the king.[13] Marini undertook most of the negotiations and missions to other powers — Poland, Hungary, Venice, Burgundy and especially, France. A good discussion of Marini's work is available in The Universal Peace Organization, *written by Václav Vaněček. Vaněček also cites the work of others, notably the German lawyer and diplomat, Dr. Martin Mair, a specialist on the Wittelsbach dynasty and an admirer of King George.[14] Besides Marini and Mair, there were probably others who worked on the plan. George,*

[13] *See Urbánek,* Věk poděbradský, *IV, pp. 576-608, and Heymann, op. cit., p. 237 f., p. 299 ff.*

[14] *See F.M. Bartoš, "Návrh Krále Jiřího na utvoření svazu evropských států," in* Jihočeský sborník historický, *XII (1939) pp. 65 ff. See also Heymann, op. cit., pp. 300-30.*

11

INTRODUCTION

however, seems to have retained the authority to make final decisions himself.

In the last phases of the creation of the plan, the names of the Polish king, Casimir IV, and the Hungarian king, Matthias Corvinus (a son-in-law of George's) were publicly associated with the project. However, the Hungarian ruler did not really intend to support it. The relations between George and King Louis XI of France were most cordial. The French king made many promises but real support from France was never forthcoming, despite Marini's missions, since most of Louis' advisers were advocates of papal policy. Thus, the plan for organizing a system of international peace in 1464 foundered; but, of course, the ideal survived.

George's ambitious vision was celebrated 400 years later with the publication of his plan under the auspices of the Czech Academy. This edition is reprinted here. In 1964 also, the Academy of Sciences in Prague held the Symposium Pragense *where numbers of foreign and Czech scholars met. Their deliberations appeared as the* Cultus Pacis *(1966).*[15] *The contributions to this volume by the French scholar, Victor L. Tapié, and particularly by the Polish authority, Roman Heck, have done much to clarify the roles played by their respective nations in the fifteenth century with regard to the peace*

[15]Cultus Pacis: Etudes et documents du "Symposium Pragense" 1464-1964, *published by the Czechoslovak Academy of Sciences, Prague, 1966.*

12

INTRODUCTION

plan.[16] *Indeed, it now seems that without the Polish commitment, the entire project might never have developed at all. Professor Heck identified the significant contribution made by the Polish statesman and thinker, Jan Ostrorog, and clearly traced the development of Polish-Czech relations from 1461-1464. While close relations of the two West Slav nations had not been common and did not survive into the modern era, perhaps the cooperation demonstrated in* The Universal Peace Organization *and the* Cultus Pacis *can guide and inspire the future.*

F. G. Heymann
Department of History
University of Calgary
Alberta, Canada

---

[16] *For his earlier studies, see Roman Heck, "Czeski plan związku wladców europejskich z lat 1462-1464 a Polska"* in Studia z dziejów polskich i czechoslowackich, *I, Wroclaw, 1960; in the publication of* Cultus Pacis, *Heck's contribution is entitled, "Polen und das Friedensprojekt Georgs von Podiebrad," pp. 97-107.*

THE UNIVERSAL PEACE ORGANIZATION OF KING GEORGE OF BOHEMIA
A FIFTEENTH CENTURY PLAN FOR WORLD PEACE
1462 / 1464

PUBLISHING HOUSE
OF THE CZECHOSLOVAK ACADEMY OF SCIENCES
PRAGUE 1964

INITIUM FOEDERIS, QUOD GEORGIUS, BOHEMIAE REX,
PERPETUAE PACIS CONSTITUENDAE GRATIA PROPOSUIT

(Warszawa, Archiwum główne akt dawnych, Metryka koronna, tomus XI, pag. 578)

PROBABLY A PORTRAIT OF KING GEORGE.
A DETAIL OF THE ALTAR-PIECE
"SALOME OFFERING THE HEAD
OF JOHN THE BAPTIST TO KING HERODES"
ON THE FOLDING ALTAR AT ZÁTOŇ

(National Gallery, Prague)

THE ALTAR-PIECE
"SALOME OFFERING THE HEAD
OF JOHN THE BAPTIST TO KING HERODES"
WITH THE PROBABLE PORTRAIT
OF KING GEORGE ON THE FOLDING
ALTAR AT ZÁTOŇ

(National Gallery, Prague)

The United Nations Educational, Scientific and Cultural Organization [UNESCO] *accepted in 1962 the proposal submitted by the Delegation of the Czechoslovak Socialist Republic that the anniversaries of outstanding personalities and historical events marked in 1964 include the 500th anniversary of the proposals which the Czech King George of Poděbrady drew up and for whose realization he strove in the years 1462-1464 in order to rid mankind of the scourge of war and to safeguard a lasting Peace throughout the World.*

‖ SCIMUS, QUOD ... LAUDI NIL GLORIOSIUS EFFICERE POTERIMUS, QUAM DARE OPERAM, QUOD VERA, PURA ET FIRMA PAX, UNIO ET CARITAS INTER CHRISTIANOS FIAT ... ; AD QUAS ETIAM RES OMNES POPULI, OMNES NATIONES OMNESQUE REGES ET PRINCIPES LAETIS ET PROMPTIS ANIMIS DEBENT ET TENENTUR INTENDERE. ‖

(From the preamble to the project of King George)

CONTENTS

Václav Vaněček, Historical Significance of the Peace Project of King George of Bohemia and the Research Problems Involved — 9

Tractatus pacis toti christianitati fiendae, *edidit Jiří Kejř*
Editorial Note
English Translation (*Ivo Dvořák*)
Russian Translation (*L. P. Mozhanskaya, E. V. Tarabrin*)
French Translation (*Konstantin Jelínek*)
Spanish Translation (*Eva Šimková*)

Czechoslovak Academy of Sciences

THE UNIVERSAL
PEACE ORGANIZATION
OF KING GEORGE
OF BOHEMIA

A *Fifteenth*
Century Plan
for World Peace
1462/1464

Czechoslovak Academy of Sciences

Scientific Editors:

FRANTIŠEK KAVKA, PHDr., CSc.
Professor of History at Charles University, Prague

VLADIMÍR OUTRATA, JUDr.
Professor of International Law at Charles University, Prague

JOSEF POLIŠENSKÝ, DrSc.
Professor of History at Charles University, Prague

PUBLISHED IN CO-OPERATION WITH THE CZECHOSLOVAK COMMISSION FOR UNESCO

THE HISTORICAL SIGNIFICANCE
OF THE PEACE PROJECT
OF KING GEORGE
OF BOHEMIA
AND THE RESEARCH
PROBLEMS INVOLVED

by Václav Vaněček, DrSc.

PROFESSOR OF HISTORY OF STATE AND LAW
AT CHARLES UNIVERSITY, PRAGUE, CORRESPONDING MEMBER
OF THE CZECHOSLOVAK ACADEMY OF SCIENCES

English translation by Ivo Dvořák, JUDr., M. A.

The most timely question we must ask ourselves when contemplating the future of mankind is how to ensure lasting peace among nations. Reviewing the history of international law and relations, a complexity of very old problems emerges which has captured the interest of statesmen, philosophers, lawyers and diplomats alike throughout the centuries.[1]

Old projects and plans for eliminating war and preserving peace were viewed with complacency by historians until recent times. They aroused nothing more than historical curiosity and at best were regarded as interesting *utopias*, noble in spirit but quite unrealistic. The turning point came only in the 20th century. We live in an era when old, utopian ideas are being realized and this has made us far more aware of bold ideas and plans conceived in remote times.

A typical example in this respect is the project of a universal peace organization which King George of Bohemia initiated 500 years ago, and for whose realization serious, now almost forgotten, diplomatic negotiations took place between European states in the years 1462—1464.

This project occupies a place of special significance in the history of peace efforts and world organizations. Not only was it the first proposal for solving these problems ever to be officially submitted and discussed, but — and this is something which we have come to appreciate especially today — it was also a project many of whose ideas have survived the centuries and are still alive today. We have come to realize the historical greatness of the project, initiated in Bohemia and supported by Poland and Hungary, and briefly also by France and Venice, only in the 20th century, when the principles which the mighty of the world began to discuss for the first time in those days are increasingly being put into effect in practical international relations.

1]   See the compilation of studies contained in *La Paix*, I—II, Bruxelles, 1961—1962, Recueils de la Société Jean Bodin pour l'histoire comparative des institutions, No. XIV—XV. — See also L. LEDERMANN, *Les précurseurs de l'organisation internationale*, Neuchâtel, 1945, the bibliography on pp. 165—173; S. J. HEMLEBEN, *Plans for World Peace Through Six Centuries*, 3rd edition, Chicago, 1945, the bibliography on pp. 195—222; E. REIBSTEIN, *Völkerrecht. Eine Geschichte seiner Ideen*, I, Freiburg—München, 1958, the bibliography on pp. 610—640. — V. VANĚČEK, „Eine Weltfriedensorganisation nach den Vorschlägen des böhmischen Königs Georg von Podiebrad und nach den Ideen des Johannes Amos Comenius", *Sitzungsberichte der deutschen Akademie der Wissenschaften zu Berlin, Kl. für Philosophie, Geschichte, Staats-, Rechts-, und Wirtschaftswissenschaften*, 1962, No. 3, Berlin, 1963.

The forthcoming 500th anniversary of the decisive step taken by King George for the realization of this project in the spring of 1464 offers the most fitting opportunity for us to try to throw as much light as possible on all that is still vague about this remarkable historical document. In the nine chapters of this study we shall try — proceeding from the existing stage of historical research — to provide at least a starting point and the essential background for greater understanding of King George's project, being fully aware not only of the general lack of knowledge regarding the issues involved, but also the exceptional complexity and difficulty of the given problems.

One of the most difficult tasks is to outline in general the spiritual trends of the era in which the project was drawn up. In the middle of the 15th century the progressive forces in Europe had already gained their first experience in the struggle which for them was primarily one for better Christianity and for a reform of the Church; as we see it, the struggle was already aimed at breaking up the system of medieval authorities, scholastic methods, hierarchies, unrealistic organizational dogmas and defunct social schemes; in some cases (the Hussite movement in Bohemia) it was actually directed against the very feudal system of which the Church was the mainstay and foremost representative.

The middle of that remarkable century was characterized by a growing number of men whose actions were dominated by the realization that the existing order of the Christian society suffered from many serious imperfections and shortcomings which prevented the society from progressing in its own interest; that interest, we should add, was mostly understood in mystical terms. These men included the secular and ecclesiastic statesmen of Christian Europe, philosophers, lawyers and theologians, in particular all those whom we may identify as spokesmen of the burghers and the peasantry. They spoke openly of a decline of Christianity and of the necessity to find appropriate means of reform. The advance of Islam from the southeast and in particular — in 1453 — the fall of Constantinople and the destruction of the Byzantine Empire by the Turks seemed to confirm that school of opinion which had claimed for quite some time that the existing concept of an all-Christian commonwealth as a theocratic monarchy was unrealistic and did not offer a guarantee either of a just order within the commonwealth or — and even less so — of its proper defence against outside forces. The declining authority of the Emperor and the Pope, as understood under the universalist theory of the two swords, was contrasted by the steadily growing authority and power of those rulers who represented the concrete power and government in the individual countries and thus laid the foundations for the creation of the system of sovereign national states in the coming centuries. Already at that time the European public opinion viewed the Emperor and the Pope simply as *ficta nomina, picta capita*, who were neither respected nor obeyed (*nulla reverentia, nulla obedientia*).[2]

This situation was reflected differently in the individual social media and interest groups,

---

2]   Roman HECK, "Czeski plan związku władców europejskich z lat 1462—1464 a Polska", in *Studia z dziejów polskich i czechosłowackich* (The Czech Plan of a Union of European Rulers from the Period 1462—1464 and Poland, in: Studies from Polish and Czechoslovak History), I, Wrocław, 1950, p. 155, footnote No. 1, which quotes the statement of Aeneas Silvius Piccolomini (subsequently Pope Pius II) made in 1454.

ranging from literary expressions of dissatisfaction and criticism to revolutionary movements of such a nature and scope as the Hussite movement. Ways and means were sought everywhere for attaining a basic turn in the existing development.

In the very heart of Europe, in Bohemia, these general trends manifested themselves in the 1460's in a manner which fully conformed to the specific conditions prevailing in that country at that time, especially if we consider the then international situation.[3] It was in this area that conditions for the formulation of a plan for a new organization of Christendom (*respublica christiana*) were especially good. It should be recalled that the Slav nations had never viewed the mediaeval empire (*imperium Romanum*) as a promoter of peace, but rather as an instrument of oppression and even annihilation, and that the Czech State had been threatened in its very existence by the old form of the all-Christian community ever since the time of Charlemagne. Moreover, not long previously — in the Hussite period — Czech political life had clashed with papal universalism in sharp conflicts which were settled only superficially and began to re-emerge in the very years in which the project was drawn up. In this period, too, King George's closest neighbour, the King of Poland, found himself in conflict with the Pope, and the general situation in Europe had reached a stage where many other countries, France in the first place, seemed to be ready to accept such a new organization of the Christian world which would do away with all that appeared to have been overcome by historical development and political reality. It was in this connection that a new system of relations between the states of Central Europe was being considered primarily between the various German principalities; such was the core of the then existing plans for the reform of the "Roman Empire" and the restoration of the imperial power.

The situation in the Czech lands, which we shall discuss in greater detail in the last chapter, has recently been well summed up by J. Polišenský: "Hussite Bohemia provided the environment where the ground was prepared for the growth of new ideas on society and the State and on relations between states."[4]

The direct stimulus which prompted the Czech proposals for the creation of a universal peace organization was the conflict with the Papal Curia in which King George found himself in the early 1460's. The conflict was provoked in 1462 by the Pope's solemn repeal of the *Compactata* agreement concluded some 30 years earlier between the Czech Hussite leaders and the Council of Basle. At the same time the Pope demanded that King George publicly renounce the agreement and restore full powers to the Catholic clergy in the Czech State, together with all Church property.

3]   The most detailed information on the international impact of King George's domestic and foreign policies can today be found in the work quoted frequently in the present study, Rudolf Urbánek, *Věk poděbradský*, IV, Čechy za kralování Jiříka z Poděbrad 1460—1464 (The Poděbrad Age, IV, Bohemia Under the Rule of King George of Poděbrady, 1460—1464), Prague, 1962, 826 pp. — An excellent survey is contained in two studies by Josef Polišenský, "Bohemia, the Turk and the Christian Commonwealth (1462 to 1620)," in *Byzantinoslavica* 14, 1953; „Problémy zahraniční politiky Jiřího z Poděbrad" (The Problems of King George's Foreign Policy), in *Acta Universitatis Palackianae Olomucencis*, Historica I, 1960 — Many valuable data on the related questions are contained in the study by R. Heck, listed in the preceding footnote. — For problems relating to the Hussite revolutionary movement see Robert Kalivoda, *Husitská ideologie* (Hussite Ideology), Prague, 1961; F. G. Heymann, *John Žižka and the Hussite Revolution*, Princeton, 1955; František Kavka, *Husitská revoluční tradice* (The Hussite Revolutionary Tradition), Prague, 1953.

4]   *Acta Universitatis Palackianae Olomucensis*, Historica I, 1960, p. 198.

At stake were the results of the Hussite revolution and the question as to whether the achievements of the Hussite reformation won by the Czech peasant armies against several Crusades, and accepted also by the moderate Hussites who had gained supremacy in the Czech State in 1434, would be preserved.

The then Pope was Pius II, a man well acquainted with Bohemia. Indeed, prior to his accession to the Papal throne, he wrote a very interesting book on the history of Bohemia under the name of Aeneas Sylvius Piccolomini. This made him all the more dangerous to King George, originally a Utraquist nobleman who first ruled the Czech State as a governor and from 1458 as its duly elected king. Today he is commonly known as the "Hussite king".

The Czech king faced the danger that the discriminatory measures applied against him by the Pope would eventually force him into political isolation, the true goal of the papal policy towards this king of heretics. King George attempted to meet this danger, among other things, by presenting the diplomacy of those days with a project which constituted one of the most interesting solutions of the burning problems which at that time disturbed all Christian Europe, as already indicated.

King George will always deserve our respect for his statesmanship which, in an international situation extremely complex, difficult and dangerous for himself and his country, made him choose and order the drafting of so grandiose and valuable a project, which must arouse admiration even today, five centuries later. The historical significance of the proposals drawn up at the court of the Hussite King also rests in the fact that their authors had by far outrun their times and indicated the proper course to be taken in the future, then still very far distant.

Although it seems unbelievable, it still remains a historical fact that in all substantial aspects this diplomatic document, originating in Prague of the second half of the 15th century, was a forerunner of all that represents the fundamentals of the world peace organization created 500 years later, in the 20th century. The League of Nations in Geneva, established in 1919 as the predecessor of the United Nations Organization which marks its 19th anniversary this year, was also designed to secure world peace, but it failed and its end was brought about by the outbreak of World War II. Thus the founding of the United Nations Organization in San Francisco after the war, in 1945, was already the second attempt in the 20th century to realize the principles which had been conceived as the only reliable basis of any organization for ensuring lasting world peace by the authors of the Czech proposals five centuries earlier.

It was only in the 20th century that mankind accepted as the basis of its supranational organization in the 1919 League of Nations Pact and the 1945 Charter of the United Nations not only the principle of peaceful settlement of international disputes, but also the principle of mutual equality of all countries associating for peaceful co-operation with maintenance of their full sovereignty; moreover, the realization of these aims also took the form of a special multilateral treaty accessible under certain conditions to all states, the whole of which was already basically contained in the project initiated at the court of King George of Bohemia 500 years ago.

Although much of the project proposed by King George in the years 1463—1464 has come into being, we realize that we are still quite far from a situation where peaceful coexistence, as the nations of the world demand it today and as it was also envisaged in King George's project —

in spite of different terminology and in connection with the social phenomena and views of those days — would become the real basis for the existence and development of human society. We should bear in mind that also then, in the early years of the second half of the 15th century, there existed, in a certain sense, two worlds, two power blocs. The Turks conquered Constantinople and uprooted the millenial Byzantine Empire, and Islam seemed to be in irreconcilable conflict with Europe and the Christian world in general, into which it was making ever deeper inroads. Nevertheless, King George's peace project did not try to avoid this obstacle. The solution it offered was quite simple. As long as Islam continued its aggression, joint defence would be organized against it; if it was prepared to make peace, the statute of the universal peace organization (dating barely ten years after the fall of Constantinople) envisaged also the possibility of peaceful coexistence with the Turks.

One of the historically most remarkable features of the new concept of world organization, behind which King George placed the full political power of this state, is the fact that the project abandoned the idea of a universal mediaeval empire (a world monarchy) headed by the Emperor and the Pope.

The document considers as the basic elements of international political life individual, independent and equal states, which is a concept generally recognized today. Thus it has been rightly stressed that King George's projects was drawn up "without regard to the decaying mediaeval traditions" (R. Urbánek).

King George was fully entitled to present such a far-reaching proposal to the leading European rulers and governments. In spite of the Pope's continued endeavour to isolate the Czech king and divide his kingdom among the neighbouring states, King George was still one of the most powerful and influential rulers in Europe. He ruled the lands of the reconstituted Crown of Bohemia, which were economically prosperous and, to a great extent, internally consolidated. He commanded one of the most powerful armies of his times, being himself an experienced and successful warrior. It is a historical fact that King George acted as mediator and arbitrator in disputes between the rulers of different neighbouring states of the Czech Kingdom. Although he was a Utraquist, he was considered fully qualified to become the *conservator pacis* in the Western Roman Empire, a possible "governor" of Germany, and the supreme commander of a joint European campaign against the Turks; he was also considered to be one of the most important candidates in the election of the new Roman king, who would rule beside the Emperor Friedrich III, and his name was mentioned in connection with the possibility of restoring the Eastern Roman Empire. Some historians believed — it is difficult to judge how far they were justified in their opinion — that King George wanted to replace the Turkish rule in Europe by Czech rule and that in his person he wanted to unify both the Eastern and Western Empire.

In any case, it would be wrong to regard King George as a daydreamer, a visionary, a utopian, a man dominated by illusions and adventurous ideas, in other words, an unrealistic thinker. Much closer to the truth are those historians who see King George as an energetic Renaissance ruler who was trying to rid himself of some outdated political concepts, a tough feudal warrior who had become battle-hardened in numerous military campaigns, but also a bold politician and statesman who thought far ahead of his times.

More than thirty years ago a German historian of law called King George's peace project a *politischer Schachzug von unerhörter Kühnheit.*[5] This is a good characteristic, but it does not portray the whole truth. There is no doubt that only a mind truly devoted to the idea of peace and humanity, a mind open to new ideas — which are traits very rarely found in monarchs — would venture in the situation in which the state he ruled found itself at that time to operate with such diplomatic skill a project of such a humanistic nature and of such historically lasting value as that which we have outlined and which we shall try to clarify in greater detail in the following chapters.

5]   W. Weizsäcker, in *Prager juristische Zeitschrift,* X, 1930, column 245.

THE CHARTER OF THE UNIVERSAL PEACE ORGANIZATION
FROM THE YEARS 1462−1464

The proposals which have thus far been characterized only in general terms were embodied in a document which may be justly called the Charter of a universal peace organization from the years 1462−1464. From the formal aspect, as indicated especially well by the newly discovered texts,[1] this document was the outline of a multilateral international treaty which in principle was open to accession by any Christian state.

The document is made up of two parts − an introduction (a preamble or a preface) and the actual proposals in the nature of an outline of the statute of the envisaged organization of European states. This organization was conceived in such a manner that eventually it might have developed into a world-wide organization.

The introduction first outlines the causes that led to the project and sets out the purposes to be achieved. It analyzes the existing state of affairs in the Christian world, stressing in particular the fact that only sixteen out of the allegedly 117 Christian states remained in being at the time of origin of the document. No explanation is given of how the authors arrived at the aforesaid figures.[2] The document speaks quite frankly of a deterioration of Christendom, whose principal cause is considered to be a lack of true unity. It was this situation that had allowed Islam constantly to bring under its power new territories which until a short time beforehand had been under Christian rule.

The document defines as the primary duty of all Christian rulers the ensuring of unity, peace

1] See *infra* on pp. 79—80.

2] Compare (according to J. Kejř) the analogical quote contained in *Tractatus de Turcis ... collectus ... a quibusdem fratribus Ordinis Predicatorum* of 1474 (printed in 1481) *impressus per Conradum Zenninger civem Nurembergensem* (Hain 15681, fol. 6a): *Nam in XXVI annis Turcus perfidus duo imperia, IIII regna, XX provincias et CC urbes suo imperio subiugavit, imperium scilicet Constantinopolitanum et Trapezuntinum. Patent ista ex oracione habita Bernardi Iustiniani oratoris Venetorum coram sanctissimo d. n. moderno summo pontifice.* (Translation: "For within 26 years the perfidious Turk subjugated under his rule two empires, namely those of Constantinople and Trapezunt, 4 kingdoms, 20 provinces and 200 cities. This is patent from the speech made by the Ambassador of Venice, Bernard Justinian, before Our Holiest Lord, the new Pontiff.")

and common defence against the penetration of Islam into Europe. In this connection invectives are heaped upon the Turks and Arabs as representatives of Islamic expansion; the lack of diplomatic tact is quite obvious today, but we must take our minds back to the situation prevailing in Europe one decade after the fall of Constantinople in order to understand and excuse this non-diplomatic bluntness.

However, the most important passages of the introduction do not mention the fight against the Turks at all. On the contrary, the document underlines the need of a united organization for the purpose of preserving peace, which is the subject of the specific proposals contained in the principal articles of the second part of the document, which represents the actual core of the whole project.

The wording of this second part outlines with remarkable clarity the main features of the universal organization of Christian states proposed by King George. It offers quite specific, concrete proposals which in some instances are worked out in considerable detail, while elsewhere they simply suggest fundamental principles. The skill and foresight of the authors are indicated by the fact that a number of questions were left open to decision by the leading organs of the future organization, with the often repeated reference: *prout subscripta nostra congregatio vel maior pars eiusdem concluserit* or similar words.

The second part of the project, that is the actual statute of the peace league, is made up of 23 articles which are arranged in a characteristic order. If we follow their contents, we cannot but notice that prime stress is laid on those dispositions which are of a political nature and involve certain social functions, being designed to bring about profound changes in interstate relations, while provisions of an organizational or even administrative nature are relegated to a subordinate position.

The most prominent place is occupied by proposals whose purpose was to exclude war from human society. This purpose is openly and exclusively followed in the first eight articles, that is, the whole of the first third of the project; these articles contain very detailed and complex regulations designed to eliminate wars, to settle disputes between states peacefully, and to punish those who disturb peace. War against the Turks is not mentioned once.

The next three articles deal with the organizational aspect of settling political conflicts without the use of force. They centre on the proposal to establish an international court of justice within the framework of the universal peace organization. This institution is defined as *generale consistorium* or simply *iudicium*. The term *parlamentum* does not appear in these three articles, although it is used in other articles with reference to the court. In this connection the document also envisages the creation of a universally applicable law.

The next Article (12) is concerned with an especially important question, namely the admission of new members to the universal peace organization.

The two following articles (13 and 14) are devoted to a problem which was of vital significance for 15th century Christian Europe, namely defence against the expansion of Islam, carried out by the Turks, and the organizational and material aspects of such defence. It was assumed that all the detailed provisions concerning the war against the Turks would be made *communi sententia totius congregationis vel maioris partis eiusdem*, including the time element, the direction of attack, the appointment of the commanders, etc.

However, as already pointed out, even in this case war was not considered unavoidable. The document envisages expressly that peace with the Turks could be made under a joint decision of the peace organization, but only if the safety of Christians living in the proximity of the Turkish realm were safeguarded (*securitas finitimorum christianorum*). Article 15 represents a financial and administrative annex to the provisions of the two preceding articles.

From the viewpoint of the history of the organizational forms of human society, the most important part of the project lies in the last eight articles. They provide a fitting formula for an organization of the human community which on one hand would fully respect the sovereignty of the individual states, both large and small, and, on the other hand, would permit the formulation of their common will for the purposes defined in the preceding articles. It is a remarkable formula in that it was rediscovered and realized only after the lapse of 500 years, in the 20th century.

Article 16 proposes the establishment of a universal peace organization made up of delegates furnished for this purpose with a very extensive authority by their respective governments. It was not to be a supranational state, but an international organization based on a multilateral treaty concluded by sovereign and equal states. This is manifest from the wording of Article 16, which briefly, but most tellingly — to a historian of law — outlines the structure and nature of this new and ingeniously conceived legal body.

The article leaves no doubt that the universal peace organization (*unio*) as proposed by King George and his allies, was to be a legal entity (*corpus, universitas seu collegium verum*) whose principal organs would have been: the assembly of delegates (*congregatio*), the council of rulers (*consilium*), an international court of justice (to which Article 16 refers in the sentence regarding its jurisdiction, see Articles 9 to 11), and an administrative apparatus which is not uniformly defined, but which today would certainly be called a secretariat. Article 16 mentions expressly a syndic (*sindicus*, who today would probably be called the secretary general), a fiscal procurator (who was to be mainly in charge of the financial backing of the organization), a treasury and archives, and other officials (*officiales*). Similarly as any organization of this kind, the universal peace organization was also to have its own coat-of-arms and seal.

The remaining articles (17 to 23) describe the structure of the universal peace organization in greater detail, in particular as regards the formulation of its common will (that is the voting procedure) and the provision of its finances (contributions to joint expenditures). Very important in this respect are the provisions of Article 21, which formulate the views of the Czech Court on the Pope's role in mobilizing the financial resources of the Church and in safeguarding peace among the Christians *vis à vis* the war with the Turks.

Against the background of still purely mediaeval phenomena and institutions (*respublica christiana*, the offices of *imperator* and *papa*, the feudal hierarchy of monarchic titles, *nationes* in the sense of regional interest groups, *oratores, decimae, salvus conductus*, etc.) we can already discern the outlines of political institutions and principles of international coexistence of a completely new character; these include primarily the proposed organization (*unio*) as such, all its basic organs (*congregatio, consilium, consistorium*), the principle of the equality of states under international law, the principle of pacific settlement of international conflicts, the express condemnation of wars, the outlawing of aggressors, the principle of collective security, etc.

Thus, thirty years before the discovery of America, the stormy events of 15th century European politics brought forth a project outlining the principles of a relationship between states, pertaining to the future. Taken as a whole — and considered in all its consequences — the project outlined the principles and features of a universal peace organization which was considered *utopian* until the 20th century. Many of the component parts of the organization are quite naturally still marked in their details, formulations and individual clauses by the views and institutional forms prevalent at the time of its origin, i.e. the late Middle Ages. King George's project was, after all, the outgrowth of its times, characterized by the complexity of the relations between rulers of different ranks and categories, and in this connection — taking into account conditions which are quite alien to us today — it tried to alleviate, through formulations most adequate five centuries ago, the burning problems of its times and to eliminate wars and other international conflicts in their contemporary forms. In this sense the complex situation of late mediaeval Europe is especially well reflected in Articles 6, 7 and 8 (see pp. 72—73), which deal with the punishment of those who disturb peace.

Even though we must constantly bear in mind, when interpreting King George's project, that a superficial, vulgar and forced comparison with modern times, to which a historian may tend in an endeavour to explain the project in terms understandable to present-day man, represents a considerable danger to the presentation of a historically true picture, we cannot but note that the project offered opportunities until then quite unknown in that form.

Mankind of the 15th century was shown the prospects of a world without wars in which even the apparently insurmountable antagonism between the Christians and Moslems appeared to be replaceable by a situation for which we can hardly find a more fitting, modern-day term than "peaceful coexistence". This is clearly indicated by the final part of Article 13 (on p. 74), which expressly envisages the possibility of peace between Christendom and the Turks.

Today, five centuries after the drafting of King George's project and its failure, we cannot but admire the boldness with which this plan of a universal peace organization was not only conceived, but also presented — and this must be particularly stressed — to the 15th century diplomatic world at the truly highest level. We have come to realize that completely novel ideas, inseparably linked with the organizational scheme of their realization, permeate the mosaic-like maze of formulas, clauses, turns of speech and legal and theological phrases common in 14th and 15th century Europe and formally proceeding from the Bible, the principles of Christian ethics, and Roman law. Lasting universal peace was to be guaranteed by the authority of a voluntary union, or league, of free, mutually independent and formally equal states, irrespective of their inner structure, form of government, etc.

It is precisely through the fact that King George's project envisaged as the contractual parties not the feudal lords in the sense of the then common domestic peace treaties (Landfrieden), but independent states represented by their rules, which were to form, under a treaty, a higher political body previously unknown in political practice, that this draft of a multilateral international treaty, negotiated on a diplomatic level in the years 1462—1464, differed basically from the usual mediaeval peace treaties, as analyzed on numerous occasions by historians of law.[3]

It is certainly no overstatement to say that King George's project, conceived in the storms and conflicts of the Middle Ages, draws, in the sphere of ideas on the organization of the world, the outlines — even though cloaked in 15th century garb — of a body which had formerly been known in a certain analogy to the people of Europe only in the form of the ideal Christian commonwealth of the early Middle Ages, which, as time has proved, was an utterly unrealistic form, based on principles of the nature of dogmas and on sanctions which were more or less mystic in character.

3] See Joachim GERNHUBER, "Staat und Landfrieden im deutschen Reich des Mittelalters", in *La Paix*, II, 1961, pp. 27—77.

The political body which was to be created under the project was not to be a supranational state and even less so a monarchy. It was to be an international organization which the Charter calls *unio* in the concluding words of its preamble; however, it also indicates its purpose and functions in the expressions *connexio, pax, fraternitas et concordia.* We shall certainly not be mistaken if we keep to the term *unio*, which describes perfectly the essence of the project, in particular since its use in the Charter itself is further documented in Articles 3 (*pax et unio praemissa*), 8 (*praesens nostra unio*), 12 (*praesens haec unio*) and other places (Articles 13 and 19). This expression can be translated either as union or unity, or finally, as is done most often in the present study, simply as organization.

Some of the phrases used in the document indicate that the authors sometimes also used the word *pax* to describe the new international body, which is reminiscent of the old tradition of medi-aeval domestic peace treaties and the Church institution of "God's Peace".[1] This is true of Articles 6, 7, 8 and 12. Once the document uses (in Article 22) the term *pax et ordinatio* by which the authors apparently meant, just as in the case of the term *foedus* (Articles 4, 5, 11, 19, 21), the formal aspect of the creation of the new organization, that is the treaty and the actual Charter.

Proceeding from the effect the organization was to have on political life, the whole entity is sometimes also described as *fraternitas* (in Article 5, *principes fraternitati nostrae non incorporati,* and in Articles 12 and 19), *caritas* (Articles 12 and 13), and *amicitia* (Article 19).

In view of its legal nature, Article 16 twice uses the expression *collegium* to describe the whole organization (*habet etiam dictum collegium*), which is also repeated in Article 19. This use is closely linked with the expression *corpus* also appearing in the said Article. Once (in Article 13) we find

---

1]   See several contributions in *La Paix*, I—II, 1961—1962, in particular, as regards domestic peace treaties, the study by J. GERN-HUBER, quoted in the preceding footnote, and, with respect to "God's Peace", the treatises by Egied I. STRUBBE, "La paix de Dieu dans le Nord de la France" (I, 489—502) and by André JORIS, "Observations sur la proclamation de la Trêve de Dieu à Liège à la fin du XIe siècle" (I, 503—545).

the term *intelligentia* which in those days was used quite commonly for international agreements in general.

Under Article 16, the plenipotentiaries of the founding states were to establish the new organization as a legal body *sui generis*. This is well documented in the words: *qui omnes ibidem ... nostris et aliorum incorporatorum seu incorporandorum nominibus corpus, universitatem seu collegium verum faciant, constituant et repraesentent.* In this respect the nature of the proposed body is still better indicated in the concluding part of the same Article, which says that, in addition to the specifically listed attributes, the organization should further possess *quaecumque alia iura ad licitum et iustum collegium quomodolibet pertinentia et spectantia.*

The legal construction used is derived from Roman law. It is closely linked with terms transposed into the Justinian codification from classical Roman jurisprudence, as witnessed by a comparison with the fragment from Gaius's *Institutions* contained in the *Digesta*.[2] We do not know whether the authors of King George's project consulted directly the *Corpus iuris civilis*, or whether they referred to one of the mediaeval handbooks of Roman law, but it is certain that the concepts and terminology of the "learned laws" of the Middle Ages, that is, Roman law and Canon law, were well known to them, as will be shown below in other examples.

It is not merely by chance that we learn in the very same Article that the proposed organization was to have its own coat-of-arms (*arma*), seal (*sigillum*), common treasury (*archam communem*), a syndic (*sindicum*) and other common institutions and officials whom we shall not discuss at this point. The above-cited fragment from Gaius expressly comments on the corporate type of legal entities:

> *Quibus autem permissum est corpus habere collegii ..., proprium est ad exemplum rei publicae habere res communes, arcam communem et actorem sive syndicum, per quem, tamquam in re publica, quod communiter agi fierique opporteat, agatur fiat.*[4]

It should be noted that under the provisions of Article 16, the member states were to be "incorporated" in the new organization. This indicates that the body which was thus to be created was to have the character of a legal entity, but no longer in the sense of private Roman law, whose principles were used in the project *per analogiam*, but in the sense of the then emerging international law. We cannot but reach the same conclusion from the rules listed in Article 12 which govern the admission of new member states to the organization. This matter was to be decided by the permanent congress of delegates (*congregatio*), which would accept from a new member a written

---

2] *Dig.* III, 4, 1, where we find not only the terms *corpus* and *collegium*, but also other terms and institutions appearing in King George's project (*arca, sindicus*).

3] Markgraf, *Historische Zeitschrift*, 1869, interprets this term as *gemeinsame Lade*, which is, of course, also a possible explanation (see *infra* in footnote No. 13).

4] Translation: "Those then, who are permitted to be organized as a *collegium* ..., shall be characterized by common property as a community, a common treasury, a representative or syndic, through whom shall be done, just as in a community, all that should be done in common."

pledge to observe the rules of the organization and which then would formally notify the governments of all the existing member states of the admission of a new state to the organization.

By concluding the treaty establishing the new organization, or by joining it subsequently, the member states would have undertaken far-reaching obligations with respect to the new political body and its new, historically unprecedented functions and jurisdiction. This was especially true as regards the questions of peace and war, of which we shall speak in detail in the next chapter, the sphere of judicial competence, finances (or, more broadly, the economic sphere), and in general, the legal sphere, since the organization was to have the exclusive right to issue generally binding legal provisions.

One of the most serious restrictions is contained in Article 22 under which the member states were to undertake the obligation to prevent by joint measures the taking of power in any of the member states by a government which would not intend to observe the provisions of the Charter. The successor of a deceased ruler was not to be allowed to ascend to the throne unless he reaffirmed in writing the obligations of his State towards the organization.

Of extreme importance was the fact that the member states were to be equal. This was the exact opposite of the ideas of the hierarchical arrangement of the Christian society prevalent in the earlier Middle Ages. We must particularly stress in this connection that nowhere in the project is mention made of any possible priority of the Roman Emperor. This ruler was apparently to be only one of the many "princes of Germany" (Article 19).

The then current theory of the superior status and power of the Emperor, or even the Pope, was not taken into account anywhere, either, as regards honorary prerogatives (a priority position) or the offices established in the international community, for example, the presidency of the organization, judicial or arbitration offices.[5] Although the Charter did not specify so expressly, there was no doubt that the proposed organization was contrary[6] to the existing concept of the Christian community headed by the Emperor and the Pope. It completely abandoned the theory of the two swords.

As for the Pope, it seems that he was not expected to become a member of the organization, just as the project apparently did not envisage the membership of the ecclesiastical princes; this fact may be viewed as one of the Hussite features of King George's project. However, the project appealed to the Pope for assistance in case the organization were to decide to take large-scale joint action against the Turks. In such case the Pope was to invite all the Christian powers, irrespective of whether they belonged to the organization or not, to participate in the action; he was also to levy a Church tax (to be drawn from the Church's extensive property) and, in general, to mobilize all Christendom. King George intended to assign to the Pope a special task in organizing a naval power against the Turks in the Italian ports.

5] See Jean GAUDEMET, "Le rôle de la papauté dans le règlement des conflits entre États aux XIIIe et XIVe siècle", *La Paix*, II, 1961, pp. 79—106.

6] See *infra* on p. 59 that contemporary observers thought the statement was heretic.

From the organizational point of view, not all the articles of the project are of the same importance, and often the questions which are of particular interest to us today are not elaborated in such detail as might have been expected. Relatively, most detailed are the provisions concerning the permanent assembly of delegates of the member states (*congregatio*), the international court (*consistorium* or *parlamentum*), and the financing of joint enterprises. Very brief and consequently vague, even enigmatic, are, for example, the provisions concerning the president of the organization, the council of rulers (*consilium*) and the higher and lower-rank officials. We must simply accept this fact. It would in no case be proper either to blame the authors for this omission or — after the lapse of 500 years — to try to interpret and supplement the project along the lines of a commentary on present-day legislation, to fill in the gaps, iron out the contradictions, or to explain dogmatically all that is vague, incomplete or even missing. We must bear in mind that we are studying a project which was never realized or even discussed at the forum where its authors had envisaged its consideration and where it could have been changed considerably; therefore we can hardly speak of its completeness or "final" version.

In the everyday practice of the new international life envisaged by King George in his project the principal organ of the proposed union was the permanent body, congress or simply assembly of delegates of the member states,[7] consistently defined as *congregatio* in the text of the project. The supreme jurisdiction of this body is documented in most of the articles, which outline quite clearly and specifically the congregation's duties. This is true especially of Articles 4, 5, 9, 11 (where its legislative function is especially marked), 12, 13, 14, 15, 16, 18, 22 and 23 (which contain a general clause defining the congregation's power to issue decisions which were to be binding for all member states).

The project does not envisage the attendance of the individual rulers at the sessions of the congregation. They were to be represented (Article 16) by their *oratores, notabiles et magnae auctoritatis viri*, furnished with full powers, that is by special delegates appointed from among persons who enjoyed the highest respect in each individual country. However, the decisions issued by the congregation were to be binding on the member states just as if they had been issued by the respective heads of state.

The congregation was to be in permanent session, but was to change its seat every five years on the basis of a specific rotation system. For the first five years it was to sit in Basle, for the next five-year period in a French city, after which it was to move to Italy, then return to Basle, etc.

In order to create a common will in this principal organ of the union, the project proposed that the member states be associated in regional groups called *nationes*. Article 19 provisionally names a French, German, Italian and, as a matter of possibility a Spanish *natio*. Each was to have *unam vocem*, a single vote in the assembly. This was a principle which King George had most probably adopted from the Church Councils where it was introduced at the beginning of the 15th century (it was used for the first time at the Council of Constance). Within each regional group, as expressly

7]   This body was aptly described as a "permanent congress of delegates" by the Czech professor international law A. Hobza in his *Úvod do mezinárodního práva mírového* (Introduction to International Peace Law), I, 1923, p. 215.

provided, each ruler (king, prince, etc.) was to have only one vote, even if he was represented by a large delegation.

The project does not mention either England or Poland, Bohemia or Hungary, not to speak of other states. Most probably, England was to be included in the "Gallic" group, while Poland, Bohemia and Hungary would have come within the "German" bloc which — as King George had hoped — could have been dominated from Bohemia as at the time of King Charles IV. In any case, at that time the term *Germania* did not mean Germany as such, but was a general, geographical term equivalent to what is today called Central Europe.

The detailed provisions of Article 19 define a complicated voting procedure in rather precise terms, so that the reader can obtain a clear picture of the proposed system of voting either from the Latin original of the project or one of its translations included in this publication. The majority system (*maior pars*) definitely prevails and only in the case of a split vote within the regional groups (*nationes*) would the political power and importance (*merita et dignitas*) of the member states and their rulers also find application.

Until new sources are discovered, the duties and functions of the council (*consilium congregationis*) which is mentioned in two places must necessarily remain obscure. Judging from the wording of Article 16 (*proprium et speciale consilium*), which states clearly that the members of the council (*membra*) were themselves to be personally the rulers of all the member states, it may be assumed that the council was to convene only occasionally and that perhaps its function was to be only of a ceremonial and auxiliary character. This seems to be supported by the fact that only in this connection do we learn of the personal head of the whole organization, who is defined as *praesidens, pater et caput*. It is generally assumed that this office would have been entrusted to the King of France. The assumption is based on the fact that Article 19 places *Gallia* first when listing the member states and the individual regional groups.

The *consilium congregationis* is also mentioned in Article 18 as the organ to which the financial contributions of the individual members should be paid, which leads us to assume that the council was to have at least some sort of a permanent secretariat attached to the congregation. But this takes us into the realm of speculation where we necessarily find ourselves every time we try to imagine in greater detail the status and functions of the president and the council and their relationship to the congregation. Since the congregation, as a permanent body, was to be composed of representatives of the individual rulers, while the rulers themselves were to govern their respective countries, we may assume that the congregation was to have been presided over by the chief delegate of the country whose ruler presided over the council. Another possibility is that the congregation might have been presided over by the syndic, whom we have already mentioned and whom we shall discuss in another connection further below.

The second most important organ of the union, which the Charter defines in considerable detail, is the international court of justice, called *parlamentum seu consistorium* (at the end of Article 3), *parlamentum vel consistorium* (in Article 4), *generale consistorium* (in Article 9), and *parlamentum seu iudicium* (in Article 18). It is generally held that the use of the term *parlamentum* indicates a trend towards the tradition of the French judicial parliaments which played an important role in the struggle between the French Crown and the centrifugal forces of the powerful feudal lords in France and which had also manifested anti-papal tendencies. Everything seems to indicate that the establishment of this body was promoted especially by A. Marini, in whose proposals it played a prominent role from the very beginning, as we shall see later.

The *parlamentum seu iudicium* was to be in charge of an extensive judicial agenda assigned to the new organization (*collegium*) under Article 16. There has been much misunderstanding in literature on this subject owing to the fact that the authors failed to note properly the inner connection between the said provisions of Article 16 and the provisions of Articles 9 to 10; Article 9 states expressly that the court would act on behalf of the whole congregation: *omnium nostrorum et congregationis nostrae nomine.*

It was assumed that the court would be composed of an *iudex* and of *assessores* to be appointed by the congregation. The latter body was also to draw up the provisions of the procedural and substantive laws to be applied in the activities of the court.

The primary duty of the international court was to settle peacefully disputes both between individual member states and between member states and states which were not members of the organization. In addition, however, (as provided in Article 16), the court was also to have wide jurisdiction — unspecified in detail — over the member states and their inhabitants in general, and in particular, was to settle any dispute submitted to it by the parties. More detailed directives in this respect were to be issued by the congregation.

The provision of Article 10, stating that the court should act *simpliciter et de plano sine figura et strepitu iudicii,* that is very simply, is directly linked with the then valid provisions of Canon law.[8] The terms *iurisdictio voluntaria et contentiosa una cum mero et mixto imperio* (Article 16) are also taken from the then current theory of "learned laws".[9]

What has already been said about the organization indicates that it was also to have a large body of officials of higher and lower rank. It may be assumed that this apparatus was to be headed by the *sindicus* mentioned at the beginning of this chapter. Using terms common today, the syndic was to be the secretary general of the organization, or, to use a more historical terminology, its chancellor. Another important official named in the project was to be the *procurator fiscalis.* Just as in the case of the syndic, in his case, too, we can find a model in Roman law[10] and in the contemporary legal and administrative practice in Italy.[11] Most probably, this official was to serve

---

8]   *Clementinarum* lib. II, tit. 1, *De iudiciis,* c. 2.

9]   *Iurisdictio voluntaria* denotes a wide field of what is known as non-contentious judicial agenda (e.g. the appointment of guardians, probate proceedings etc.), as opposed to contentious jurisdiction (*iurisdictio contentiosa*). — *Merum imperium* means higher, basically criminal jurisdiction, while *mixtum imperium* encompasses lower criminal jurisdiction together with civil jurisdiction. For the latter see K. WEIMANN, "Das tägliche Gericht" in *Gierke's Untersuchungen,* No. 119, Breslau, 1913, pp. 76, 83. This division, too, is based on the provisions of Justinian's *Corpus iuris civilis,* 1. 3 D. de iurisd. II, 1.

10]   Compare with *procurator Caesaris,* e.g. in *Dig.* XLIX, 14, *De iure fisci.*

11]   E.g. at the Papal Curia there was a *procurator fiscalis* in 1462, *Fontes rerum Austriacarum,* 2. Abt., XX, 1860 (Palacký, *Urkundliche Beiträge*), p. 269. — In Bohemia, the existence of a royal procurator was proved in and after 1453.

as a guardian of legality inside the organization. Under Article 18 he was to have the duty and the right (in addition to the syndic) to enforce payment of membership contributions, both by reminder and by action in the court of the organization, as well as by execution *manu militari* on the basis of a judgment issued in the name of the organization.

The fact that there were to be other officials, too, is documented not only by the general mention of *officiales* in the final part of Article 16 and the mention of *collectores* in Article 18, but also by the provision establishing the *archivum publicum* at the end of Article 16. In view of the fact that Article 18 assumes that the contributions would be paid by the members *ad archivum publicum*, many authors[12] have expressed the opinion that this institution was simply the treasury of the organization. We believe that it may have been a combination of an accounting office and treasury. The final answer to this question may be found after a thorough study of the early history of modern administrative practices.

As regards the official apparatus, the project includes a very interesting provision (Article 18) stating that the higher official posts (*potiora officia*) were always to be held primarily by men from the countries of the area (*de eadem natione*) where the congregation momentarily had its temporary seat. We may assume from this provision that the administrative apparatus of the organization would have undergone considerable changes after every five years.

As for the financial coverage of the costs of the organization, which even in this connection include "maintenance of peace" in the first place, the member states were to pay under Article 18 regular contributions to the treasury of the organization. Their amount was determined in a way that seems rather unusual to us. Unless we are mistaken, the payments were based on the three-day proceeds of annual financial receipts of every state.[13] The organization was to receive 10 per cent (*decima pars*) of this sum. The collection and the enforcement of the payment of the contributions were to be secured by the measures mentioned above.

In addition, in Article 4, the project envisaged the payment of special financial contributions by member states for the benefit of a member who had been forced to defend himself against unprovoked attack. The project is very specific in this respect, even though its provisions are quite complicated. Article 13 specifically applies this general principle to a situation in which an attack would be made on some Christian states. In this respect the project adds the proposal that the individual member states donate to the attacked — besides the normal contributions (*ut praefertur*) — also all the tithes belonging to the Church. This proposal is supported by the provisions of Article 21 (*exactio praedicta, decima praefata*), which calls on the Pope to ensure the expeditious and full realization of such aid.

In addition to and in connection with the maintenance of peace, the organization was to have devoted its attention to a number of other, very important and practical common matters. Perhaps

12] MARKGRAF, *op. cit.* 1869, p. 283, and his followers.

13] Beginning with MARKGRAF (*op. cit.*, pp. 282—283), these fiscal proposals are interpreted in literature in many ways. However, we believe the general principle is much more important than the exact details of a juridical system.

the most interesting proposals in this respect are included in Article 14, within the general framework of the plan for common defence against the Turkish threat. The article envisages the possibility of the organization having its own coinage (*communis moneta*) as well as the establishment of a system of price controls (*victualia in competenti pretio*) and of a network of accommodation facilities (*hospitia in civitatibus, villis et aliis locis opportunis*). Although these proposals are formally connected with military objectives, there is no doubt that their consequences would have been of a more general nature. It should be realized that if the common coinage, uniform prices of food, etc., had once been established, they could not have been limited to serving exclusively for the purpose of military defence against the Turks. Should the organization have once decided to mint its own, valuable coins, the circulation of such coins could not have been limited by any edict. The provision of foodstuffs needed for the armies of the organization and the fixing of their uniform prices, as envisaged in the project, would necessarily have affected the masses of producers in a number of countries, and, finally, even the proposed network of accommodation facilities could not have been isolated in everyday practice from the other, non-military needs of the organization, or from the life of the civilian population.

A place of particular importance in the project is occupied by the duties which the authors imposed on the proposed organization in the sphere of maintenance of international peace and, in the closest connection therewith — as they expressly state — also in the sphere of law and justice in general. These duties form the subject of the next chapter.

4

PEACE AND JUSTICE — THE PRINCIPAL OBJECTIVES
OF KING GEORGE'S PROJECT

In the survey offered in Chapter 2, we pointed to the fact that more than one third of all the articles contained in the project were devoted to the endeavour to secure lasting peace. We also underlined the fact that most of these articles formed the initial part of the project (Articles 1 to 8), which stresses their importance still further.

Articles 1 to 8 logically pursue the ideas expressed in the preamble which unequivocally sets forth the thesis that the principal objective of the times is to create such a united organization of states (*regna et principatus*) as would rid the world of the scourge of wars and institute a reign of peace, fraternity and love.

There is nothing more deserving, according to the preamble, *quam dare operam quod vera, pura et firma pax, unio et caritas inter christianos fiat*, than to strive for a true, pure and lasting peace among Christians and for their unity and mutual love. The project states as the primary purpose of such a state: *ut bella, rapinae, tumultus, incendia et caedes ... cessent et penitus extinguantur ...*, namely that wars disappear from the world.

This principal idea of King George's project is briefly expressed in the beautiful words *cultus pacis*, used in Article 9 — a cult of peace, peaceful endeavour.

King George proposed to all the European states of his day that they establish *pacis ... unionem ... perpetuis temporibus duraturam*, a peaceful union which would last forever. As we have seen, the organization which was to be thus established is often called *pax*. The range of those to whom King George and the other supposed submitters of the project addressed their appeal was very broad — *omnes populi, omnes nationes, omnesque reges et principes* — the Christian nations being, of course singled out in the first place. In this respect we must not be misled by that feature of the great project, which I would venture to call "formal, Christian limitation". We must remember that the 15th century world which King George could consider as his political partner was — with the exception of the Islamic lands — a truly Christian world. As for the Moslem world, it was then represented by the Turks and, from the Christian viewpoint, it was a world of the Antichrist, a world ruled by *christiani nominis hostis saevissimus*, to quote Article 13. It is generally known that even several centuries later, when new continents had long been discovered, other peace projects, considered to be universal, were also characterized by such formal, Christian limitation.

On looking at the project from this aspect, there can no longer be any doubt that the basic and characteristic feature of King George's project was its universality, even though it was still garbed in a Christian cloak, in keeping with the then prevailing situation. It is, however, a universality of a different nature than the universality of the earlier Christian Middle Ages. The project proposed the establishment of an international commonwealth of equal nations and states which, as a unit organized under new principles, without the Pope and the Emperor, would be responsible for the maintenance of world peace, for the peaceful settlement of international conflicts, for the punishment of those who dared to disturb peace, and, in connection therewith, also for the expeditious liquidation, by joint effort, of what then appeared as the greatest and permanent threat to the peace of the then known world, namely the aggressive designs of the Turkish Sultanate.

Action against the Turks was not the main or, even less so, the only purpose of King George's project. It is quite wrong to believe — as many historians, non-lawyers, still do — that King George merely strove for another Crusade. Such interpretation is at variance with the very text of the project and even more so with the intentions of the Czech court and the general tendency of the Czech policy of those days. It is an interpretation which unjustly narrows down the purpose of the project to one of its several objectives, to an objective which, although not unimportant, was still of secondary importance.

The actual purpose of King George's project was the establishment of a new, universal organization of states belonging to the Christian community, and, in time, of a new organization of the whole world which would do away with all wars and would thus secure a life of lasting peace for all humanity. It was therefore quite fitting that when the project was sent to the King of Poland from Prague in 1463, its copy was marked in the official files of the Polish Court as *Tractatus pacis toti christianitati fiendae*.[1]

As regards the Islamic world, it should also be noted that the general situation was quite different to that prevailing at the time when a common war against the Turks was advocated in the project of Pierre Dubois. In King George's time — as the project stresses in several places — the need existed of defence against the Turks deep inside Europe, while at the beginning of the 14th century a call was made for seizing the Holy Land from the infidel. This is yet another reason why we cannot agree with those authors who view the purpose of King George's project as organizing a war effort against the Turks. Defence against the Islamic aggression in Europe was undoubtedly one of the essential tasks of the organization, but certainly not its only or final task.

Particular stress must be laid on the fact that the final part of Article 13 envisages the possibility of concluding peace even with the Turks by a common decision of the organization (*communi sententia*). In other words, under certain conditions, which are clearly specified, the authors of the project provided for the possibility of applying the principle of peaceful coexistence also towards Islam!

1]   Compare with pp. 69, 79.

On the other hand, of course, defence against the Turkish invasion of Europe offered such an effective argument for the new organization of Christendom that it simply could not be ignored in promoting the project. That is why the document applies the defence against Islam most effectively whenever it is needed as a promotion incentive, namely in some parts of the preamble and in Articles 13, 14 and 21. However, most of the actual project does not depend on this secondary objective, pursuing with remarkable consistency, boldness and foresight the main objective — the creation of a completely new and as broad an organization of states as possible which would maintain lasting peace throughout the world. We are fully justified in stating that the proposal called for an organization which was potentially universal.

Let us now devote our attention to the situation which was to be created among the member states under King George's project. Under the provisions of Article 1, the representatives of the participating states were to pledge themselves to establish a fraternity. They were to create *pura, vera et sincera fraternitas*, which is formulated in another place (Article 23) as *verae et sincerae fraternitatis vinculum*. The situation that was thereby to be instituted was simply called *pax* or *pax generalis* (Article 6). In order to ensure the maintenance of this situation on a permanent basis, the project includes the remarkable provision of Article 22, which we discussed in another connection,[2] under which the successor of any deceased ruler who was a member of the organization would not be allowed to take over the reign unless he pledged himself in writing to continue observing the statute of the organization.

What was to be the practical effect of this fraternity on international relations? The wording of King George's project is quite specific in this respect. The very first article clearly bans the use of force in the settling of disputes between the member states of the proposed organization. It is laid down that none is to resort to force of arms against the other (*nec ... mutuo ad arma veniemus*) because of any "dissension, complaint or quarrel". On the contrary, they were all to help one another against any aggressor.

This means simply that war between the member states was to be completely eliminated. Any dispute that may have arisen, was to be settled only by the regular organs of the union, as specifically provided in Article 11, which refers to the jurisdiction of the court of justice of the organization. Article 3 expressly states that even damage caused through any act, especially of a criminal character, committed by the nationals of a member state on the territory of another member state, should not be used as a pretext for abolishing the state of peace and that it should not be settled by force of arms, but by legal process, which means primarily through action in the competent courts.

Should a member of the organization be forced to defend himself against another state by war — without having provoked the attack — Article 4 provided, among others, that all the other member states should help the attacked one by special financial contributions as long as it should prove necessary.

2]   See *supra*, p. 24.

In order to avoid conflicts between member and non-members states, the project provided that war should be prevented first by mediation at the cost of the organization and *ex officio* on the part of the organs of the organization. Should this have failed, the organization would have assisted its member.

Finally, as regards war between non-member states (Article 5), the project strove to prevent it by instructing the organization to offer its good services for the purpose of mediation. This expressly applied to *alios principes et magnates christicolas fraternitati nostrae non incorporatos.* However, should war have nevertheless broken out, the organization would have supported that party, which was willing to accept its good services and thereby demonstrated its opposition to war.

These provisions were expressly warranted by the interest *ut inter reliquos Christi fideles de hoc foedere non existentes etiam pax vigeat,* namely, to maintain peace also among those states which remained outside the organization.

The use of force in international conflicts in the case of member states would have depended on the consent of the organization. This is the true meaning of the words *absque legitimo edicto,* used in Article 1, which apply to the decision (*edictum*) of the organization as to whether armed force could be used against another state.[3] Military action by a member state against another state without the consent of the organization would have constituted a breach of the Charter. This is linked with the phrase *nostrae praesentis pacis edicta,* used in Article 7, which also denotes the decision of the organization on the question of war and peace.

Thus the project contains a remarkable proposal for legally restricting one of the typical, external functions of the state, namely belligerency. There is no doubt that such an obligation undertaken by the member states would have restricted their sovereignty just as certain other provisions of King George's project, in particular those concerning the jurisdiction of the union over the member states and the admission of the successor of a deceased ruler to government.

The fundamental provisions against war, which we have just cited, were casuistically elaborated in great detail in the further provisions of King George's project so as to provide for any eventualities and to counter any possible excuses and arguments proferred by the belligerents.

Especially detailed provisions referred to cases of an actual breach of the rules by those who were to be bound by the organization as indirect participants, that is, by those who were feudally dependent on the direct members of the organization.

Disturbers of peace were to be treated as common criminals: *arrestabuntur, capientur et punientur ut violatores pacis generalis prout qualitas delicti seu excessus cuiuslibet eorum meruerit.* They were to be arrested, captured and punished, as expressly stated in Article 6. Under the same article, nobody who had broken the regulations concerning the peaceful settlement of disputes was to be granted protection and assistance in any of the member states. Any letters of safe conduct (*salvus conductus*) which may have been issued to such disturbers of peace would not have been valid (Article 7).

3] The use of the word *edictum* in this connection has an old tradition. It implies the definition of a "just war" contained already in the Etymologies of Isidor of Seville (560–636 A.D.) and also included in *Gratian's Decretum* in the 12th century ("*Iustum bellum est, quod ex edicto geritur...*"). See V. E. Hrabar, *Revue de droit international XVIII,* 1936, pp. 29, 403.

In general Article 8 provides that any person who in any way supported the disturber of peace was to receive the same penalty (*pari poena puniatur*) as the disturber himself.

In order to understand the full impact of King George's project as regards the elimination of wars, we must recall the political realities of the second half of the 15th century. Both, wars between individual states (i. e. international wars) and between individual feudal lords — the typically mediaeval "private" wars — within the same state or in different states, were the order of the day. A document dating from 1460 describes the situation in Central Europe (it speaks specifically of Germany, *Teutonia*) as follows:

> *hic civitates cum principibus lites immortales ducunt, hic princeps principi, civitas civitati bella movent, nec sit tam infimae conditionis, qui vicinis ex arbitrio bella indicere non praesumat; et inde nullus angulus Theutoniae quietus, quocumque pergamus, insidias, spolia et mortem timemus; neque pax clero, neque nobilitati honor est.*[4]

The peaceful purposes of the proposed organization are well manifested in the provisions devoted to matters of justice.

The opening part of Article 9 sets forth the thesis — let us leave aside the extent to which it is outdated by present-day theories concerning society, the causes of wars and the substance of law and justice — that the endeavour to maintain peace (*pacis cultus*) cannot exist without justice, just as justice cannot exist without peace. Of course, it is most important how we interpret the term *iustitia*. However, in any case it is quite certain that the authors of the project understood justice as the realization of law and that they were dissatisfied with the then prevalent law.

We have here very interesting evidence of social criticism which even penetrated into such a lofty and official document as King George's project. The authors primarily criticize the judicial system of their times but — as we can see — their criticism affects at the same time the whole legal order and thereby — without the authors having realized it — the whole of society.

The reform they promote and demand is of a truly revolutionary nature. The old law, they say, must be replaced by a new one, as required in the various countries by the needs of the new times (*novorum temporum*). This new law, as the project expressly notes, must be drawn from nature (*de naturae gremio nova iura producere*) and must be arranged so that it can remedy the existing social ills (*novis abusibus nova remedia*). The Norwegian historian of law Christian Lange rightly

---

4]   From the report of M. Mair to King George, Palacký, *Urkundliche Beiträge* (*Fontes Rerum Austriacarum*, 2. Abt., XX), 1860, p. 205. — Translation: "here quarrel cities with princes without end, one prince is at war with another prince, one community with another, and none is of so low a state as not to dare arbitrarily to declare war on his neighbour; and therefore no part of Germany is quiet, wherever we may turn, we must fear some treachery, robbery and death; there is no peace here for the clergy and no respect for the nobility".

noted, when speaking of these words, that they may well have come from the introduction to a 17th century treatise on natural law.[5]

We may, perhaps, accept also the interpretation that the project proposed the acceptance by all member states of the obligation to replace gradually the old law by such a new law *de naturae gremio*. However, the fact that as the first step in introducing the new law the project proposes the establishment of an international court, whose universal nature is indisputable (compare Articles 9—10 and Article 16), leads us to the conclusion that the authors of the project intended to introduce a universal law, differing from Roman law, which would apply throughout the world. This is also indicated by Article 11, which envisages that the permanent congress of delegates (*congregatio*) would issue generally binding legal regulations (*statuta, decreta et ordinationes*) for all member states. All these facts show that this is one of the boldest ideas incorporated in the project. Not so long ago it was considered to be an outright utopia.[6] It is only in recent years that we have reached the stage where a similar idea is being considered in quite serious legal works.[7]

This proposal for introducing a new law has an interesting place in the history of King George's project. It shows again how profoundly the project was influenced by A. Marini, and also how the latter's views were not accepted uncritically but, on the contrary, were criticized and changed accordingly in the final draft of the project. This draft should be compared with a characteristic passage from Marini's yet unpublished memorandum, dated 1462, which we shall discuss separately[8] and which reflects Marini's hostile attitude to contemporary jurisprudence in general and to lawyers in particular (even though he exempted contemporary lawyers from his criticism). Marini listed the three main causes of the deterioration of Christianity, sharply criticizing contemporary jurisprudence. He claimed that jurisprudence had gone astray because it had abandoned its true fundamental principles: *Omnes iuris consulti dimiserunt 12 genera legum et 4 naturas sententiarum et 3 regulas geometricales, quae totum regebant mundum.* Lawyers, says Marini, have brought such confusion into legislation and jurisprudence that they are no longer able to decide anything: *Isti iurisconsulti tantas fecerunt leges et tantos libros scripserunt, quod unus confundit alium et se soli intelligere non potuerunt. Praesentibus temporibus nesciunt discidere causas nisi post quod sunt destructae partes...*

The criticism contained in King George's project not only follows a different trend, but also points to a quite different, optimistic and constructive solution. There is no criticism of jurispru-

---

5] Christian L. LANGE, *Histoire de l'internationalisme*, I (until 1648), Oslo, 1919, Publication de l'Institut Nobel Norvégien, IV, p.114. — The essence of the term *natura* in the legal theory of the late Middle Ages is aptly explained in Jan KRČMÁŘ's *Základy Bartolovy a Baldovy teorie mezinárodního práva soukromého* (The Foundations of Bartolo's and Baldo's Theory of Private International Law), Prague, 1910, p. 142.

6] Characteristically, we can find as late as in 1941 the following sentence in the *Zeitschrift für öffentliches Recht*, XXI, p. 218: "Heute wie damals (i.e. in the Middle Ages) ist eine Menschheitsgemeinschaft mit einem ihr entwachsenen Weltrecht eine Utopie" (H J. HELD).

7] C. Wilfred JENKS, *The Common Law of Mankind*, London, 1958. A review of this book was published in the Polish journal *Państwo i Prawo* (State and Law), 1959, No. 11, pp. 876 seq.

8] See *infra*, p. 40.

dence and, indeed, the role played by lawyers in the approval of the project, whose purpose was the maintenance of peace and administration of justice, is underlined at the end of the preamble (*iuris divini et humani doctorum nostrorum ad hoc adcedente consilio et assensu*).

This fact, too, indicates that a lawyer must have played a major role in drawing up the project and corrected Marini's sharply critical view of jurisprudence. We may even say that much of the project offers a classical example of what was subsequently called *iurisprudentia architectonica*.[9]

9] Compare e.g. Debra-Neumann, *Dissertatio de commissionibus*, Prague, 1739, p. 95.

5

THE ORIGIN OF THE PROJECT
FROM AN ANTI-TURKISH ALLIANCE TO A UNIVERSAL PEACE
ORGANIZATION

There is every indication that King George's project of a universal peace organization, as we know it from the years 1463—1464, did not come into being all at once. The idea of a new commonwealth of nations to replace the outmoded universal Christian monarchy seems to have matured gradually at the royal court in Prague between 1461 and 1463. Today we are able to divide this development into two distinctive stages.

The first stage is characterized by the intention to unify the armed forces of all Christendom, or at least the major Christian powers, under the command of the Czech king for a decisive military attack on the Turks and the recapture of Constantinople; another aim was the establishment of some sort of an international court of justice (parliament) which would settle disputes arising between the members of the anti-Turkish alliance.

This plan, which seems never to have been drawn up in an official form, was initiated and promoted by Antonius Marini of Grenoble, a Frenchman in the services of King George.[1] This enterprising and exceptionally talented man of universal knowledge, who used the title of knight (*miles*) was originally a master engineer, specializing in brick-making, coal-mining and metal-lurgy (*carbonista*).[2] His name is first mentioned in historical documents in 1456, when he was granted an industrial patent in Steir by the Emperor Friedrich III. Subsequently he made his way to Prague where he attained a position of considerable importance at the Court of King George as an expert on economic — especially commercial — matters and on international affairs.

In the second stage, when the international political situation had changed in the years 1462 and 1463, Marini's original plan gave the incentive for a much broader and more grandiose scheme,

---

1]   Regarding A. Marini see in detail R. Urbánek, *op. cit.*, IV, 1962, pp. 214 *seq.* — E. Denis, *De Antonio Marini et de Bohemiae ratione politica eo oratore*, Angoulême 1878. — N. Iorga, "Un auteur de projets des croisades, Antoine Marini", in: *Études d'histoire du Moyen Age dédiées à Gabriel Monod*, Paris, 1896.

2]   In the records of the Czech mission to Rome in March 1462, Marini is characterized as *Antonius carbonista de Francia, laicus,* Palacký, *Urkundliche Beiträge*, 1860, p. 268.

the project of a universal peace organization, in whose development King George himself played a leading role. The new plan was drawn up in the form of an official diplomatic instrument with special emphasis laid on its legal aspect. Most probably it was drawn up not only by Marini, but also by another close associate of King George.

The first reliable document showing that the project was completed dates from the summer of 1463, when the text of the project was recorded in the archives of the Polish Royal Chancellery (known as the *Metryka koronna*). This, thus far the oldest known evidence of the final version of the project has been mentioned in literature only in recent years.[3] It was entered in the *Metryka koronna* on the basis of a document which King George had sent to King Casimir of Poland through Marini some time in the summer of 1463; at that time Marini was employed at the Polish Court in an official capacity, viz. as counsellor and spokesman (*consiliarius et orator*) of both King Louis XI of France and the Czech king.

This text, which is being published[4] exactly 500 years after its inclusion in the *Metryka koronna*, allows us to determine the exact wording of King George's project in many respects. The title with which it was furnished in Poland provides important evidence that the project was viewed at its time as an instrument of peace rather than war.[5] Even though it raises some problems which we are thus far unable to answer in a satisfactory manner, it greatly helps us to reconstruct the diplomatic negotiations concerning the project and, in general, the history of the concept of the universal peace organization proposed by King George.

There are numerous and convincing reasons why we may conclude that the project of a universal peace organization, as first documented in 1463, was not identical with Marini's proposals dating from the years 1461 and 1462.

Taken in chronological order, the first of Marini's proposals was contained in a few lines of a letter the Frenchman addressed to King George from Italy on August 8, 1461.[6] These lines are very typical of Marini. The Renaissance diplomat mentions in a mysterious, promising and boastful manner ("I shall show them my wits") his plan of which, as he stresses, he had informed only the Pope. He writes expressly that it will be a "thing" which will "uplift the Faith of Christ as was once done by the Gottfrieds of Bouillon". This could hardly have meant anything else — in connection with what we shall discuss later — than the organization of an all-Christian campaign against the Turks[7] in which King George was to have played an especially important role. If we

---

3] Roman HECK, *op. cit.*, p. 169, footnote No. 50. — V. VANĚČEK, *Sitzungsberichte*, 1963, p. 13 — Jiří KEJŘ, in: *Právněhistorické studie* (Studies in Legal History), IX, Prague, 1963, pp. 249 *seq.*

4] *Právněhistorické studie* (Studies in Legal History), IX, 1963, pp. 249 *seq.*

5] Compare *supra*, p. 31.

6] *Časopis Společnosti wlastenského Muzeum w Čechách* (Journal of the Society of the National Museum in Bohemia), II/3, 1828, p. 24 (ed. František PALACKÝ).

7] Palacký recognized it correctly, *ibid.*, p. 8.

compare this plan with the project from the years 1463—1464, we can see clearly that King George's proposals had quite a different political aim, a different content, and, in contrast to Marini's "witty scheme", were carefully kept secret from the Pope, and for good reasons, too.

The second reason why we cannot identify Marini's original plans with the project whose 500th anniversary we are marking ensues from a well-known passage from the introduction to an undated treatise written in the Czech language, whose author was undoubtedly Marini and which is entitled *Advice to King George on improving commerce in Bohemia*.[8] Palacký — and other historians after him — placed the origin of the *Advice* to 1463, without specifying why they did so. I believe — in connection with the arguments raised on these pages — that the *Advice* was written earlier, in 1462, either in the late summer or early autumn. I share Urbánek's views that after his journey to Venice in the summer of 1462, Marini returned to Prague and from there proceeded to Burgundy and France in the winter of 1462—1463.[9]

In the very important opening sentences of his treatise, Marini notes that King George has asked him — as his advisor — seven questions on which he wanted his expert opinion. In the first question the King asked Marini how the Czech State could restore good relations with the Roman Church. The second question, which for us is much more important, was worded as follows, if we are to believe Marini's reproduction:

> *How can all Christian princes be brought to three objectives: first, to peace and a general treaty, secondly, to have them all together defend the Faith, thirdly, to preserve the honour of the Holy Mother of the Roman Church and the Holy See and the Holy Empire.*

In his very brief reply to the first two questions (since the treatise was devoted to commerce, which was the subject of the very last, seventh question), Marini refers to his old idea, which, he claims, he had discussed with the king on several occasions and which, as he writes with obvious exaggeration, he had discussed under the king's instructions "in all Christian nations".

Marini expresses the substance of his concept in relation to the first question with the term "parliament", and in relation to the second question with the term "new parliament". Let us note right now that the term *parlamentum* does in fact appear in the project dating from the years 1463 to 1464[10] as one of the expressions used to describe the international court of justice whose establishment King George had proposed within the framework of the universal peace organization.

If the plan we know from the years 1463—1464 had already existed at the time King George posed his questions to Marini, the second question would not have made much sense. On the other hand, if Marini had already at that time had the grand project in mind, he could not have referred

---

8] František PALACKÝ, *ibid.*, pp. IX *seq.*; compare also the edition published in *Výbor z literatury české* (Anthology of Czech Literature), II, 1868, pp. 778 *seq.* — See also PALACKÝ, *Dějiny IV* (edited by B. RIEGER), p. 336. The most recent analysis of Marini's treatise can be found in R. URBÁNEK, *op. cit.*, IV, 1962, pp. 227 *seq.* — MARKGRAF, *op. cit.*, 1869, p. 270, did not deal with this matter in a satisfactory manner.

9] R. URBÁNEK, *op. cit.*, IV, 1962, p. 591, see also p. 581.

10] In Articles 3, 4, 18, see *infra* on pp. 71, 76.

to this old plan which, as he expressly states, he had moreover discussed with the king on many occasions and whose principal feature was, besides the all-Christian campaign against the Turks, an institution defined as "parliament".

One cannot but gain the impression that at the time he posed his questions to Marini, King George already had in mind a different, much more grandiose idea towards which all the three points raised in his second question, as reproduced above, seemed to have been directed. Foremost in this new concept was the idea of universal peace. The war against the Turks receded into the background and was expressly conceived as defence. Moreover, the idea of a *general treaty* was brought up at that time as an open, multilateral treaty; this idea was consistently applied in the 1463—1464 project as the basis of the proposed universal peace organization. Finally (as reflected in the third point raised in the second question), King George viewed as a serious and separate problem the status of the Emperor and the Pope, or the Holy Roman Empire and the Roman Church, as regards the new organization, which problem had never been raised in Marini's old proposals.

The concept which Marini had until then promoted in various European countries was a more modest one, having the nature of an anti-Turkish league associating all the major European powers and not constituting any departure from the mediaeval concept of a universal Christian monarchy headed by the Emperor and the Pope.

Quite instructive in this respect is a comparison between the final project, dating from the years 1463—1464, and the voluminous memorandum (*parva scriptura*) which Marini, who in this document called himself *Anthonius Marini Gratiopolitanus ex Delphinatu*, wrote for the Czech and Polish kings "and for all other princes and lords" in 1462.[12] In his memorandum Marini tried to analyze the contemporary, unfavourable state of the Christian world and also submitted proposals for mending the situation. The document not only shows that in 1462 Marini still viewed the aim of his plan as very limited (*fidem defendere et Turcum expellere*) but, and in particular, also that he fully accepted as the basis of his ideas the mediaeval theory of the two swords: ... *ista sunt duo capita mundi, scilicet papa in spiritualibus et imperator in temporalibus.* Marini constantly stressed the necessity of maintaining the imperial and papal authorities and decried the fact that they were not duly respected. He considered it wrong that every prince wanted to be the Emperor and the Pope in his own land. He complained that the commoners had lost their faith and obedience, that

11] Compare in particular the document from Venice, dated August 9, 1462, PALACKÝ, *Urkundliche Beiträge*, 1860, p. 289, No. 295, where the proposals discussed by Marini until then are recorded as follows: ... ... *propositum domini sui regis ac regis Pollonie ad procedendum magnanime contra Turcum* ... *Commemoravitque ligam et intelligentiam faciendam esse inter hoc principes christianos, videlicet regem Franchorum, reges ipsos Bohemie et Pollonie, regem Hungarie, ducem Burgundie, ducem Saxonie et nos dominiumque nostrum, quibus potentatibus unitis procedendum erat ad ruinam et exterminium istius communis hostis.* We should add that the *dux Saxoniae* named in the above quoted text should have read *dux Bavariae* (Urbánek, *op. cit.*, 1962, p. 583, footnote No. 24).

12] This source, which is very important as regards the origins of King George's project, can be found in the State Library at Munich and has not yet been published. It was last mentioned by R. URBÁNEK (*op. cit.*, 1962, pp. 583—590), who, however, failed to realize the fundamental difference between the political concept of the memorandum and the concept of the project dating from the years 1463 and 1464. — Before that, Marini's memorandum was mentioned by TER MEULEN, *Der Gedanke der internationalen Organisation in seiner Entwicklung 1300—1800*, the Hague, 1917, p. 109, on the basis of information found in the work of N. IORGA. However, the date he applied (1463) is incorrect.

they did not even respect their lords, etc. In order to change this situation, Marini recommended the formation of an alliance of the kings of France, Bohemia, Poland and Hungary,[13] whose outlines emerged in greater clarity following the meeting of King George and King Casimir of Poland at Głogów. The purpose of the alliance would have been primarily the consolidation of all Christian forces for the war against the Turks. Marini asked expressly that these moves should first be reported to the Pope and the Emperor who were to be assured that the objective was to restore their authority and power.

From the organizational point of view, we find that in his memorandum Marini once again applied only the "idea of an international court of arbitration" basically in the same form as it had appeared in the early 14th century in the proposals of Pierre Dubois.[14]

As we can see, the overall political trend of Marini's memorandum differed substantially from the trend manifested in the subsequent project from the years 1463—1464. However, the memorandum contains some features which are found in the project of the universal peace organization, which makes it most probable that Marini personally took part in the drafting of the final version of King George's project. In any case, there is no doubt that Marini's memorandum of 1462 was used in drawing up the preamble to the final project.

Thus, as many factors seem to indicate, the idea of a potentially universal union of sovereign states, without the Emperor and the Pope, originated at the royal court in Prague in the autumn of 1462. I believe that a major role was played in this respect by King George himself. It is a matter of universal knowledge that King George did not know Latin, or at least not so well that he could express himself in it or read it as readily as the scholars of those days. This means that he must have communicated his ideas on the peace organization to his associates and aides in his native tongue, in Czech, and that, on the other hand, all that his learned advisors drew up and formulated in Latin had to be translated for him into Czech.

The main incentive for this new idea were the events which had markedly affected the domestic and foreign policy of the Czech State in the spring and summer of 1462. The abrogation of the *Compactata* by the Pope on March 31 created a new situation involving a number of burning problems. The papal move was debated in August by the Estates of Bohemia and resulted in a dangerous split between the Hussite majority and the Catholic minority. In September, the situation was discussed in Prague by a joint synod of Utraquist and Catholic clergymen, at which King George unequivocally reasserted his intention to uphold the *Compactata* as one of the mainstays of the Constitution, for which he won the praise of the Hussite party.

13] URBÁNEK, *op. cit.*, 1962, p. 590, footnote No. 39, points out that somewhat further on the memorandum says *tota vestra liga principum tam Francigenorum quam Italicorum et Germanicorum*, which he ascribes to Marini's negligence.

14] This was stressed by R. URBÁNEK, *op. cit.*, 1962, p. 589.

It was probably then, in the midst of his council, that King George conceived his plan, which went far beyond Marini's original proposals. A plan was being formulated, which was probably worked out in detail under the king's instructions by his expert advisors, to serve as the basis for further diplomatic negotiations at the European courts in the years 1463 and 1464. This question has already been touched upon by R. Urbánek, but he did not consider it in all its consequences.[15]

While in the spring of 1462, at the conference in Glogów, King George seems not to have discussed with King Casimir of Poland other matters than an anti-Turkish alliance and, perhaps, the possibility of convening a congress of European rulers for the purpose of peaceful settlement of various issues, half a year later a project was shaped at the Prague court whose objective was no less ambitious than to replace the existing, typically mediaeval ideas of a universal Christian monarchy by an idea which was to be realized only as late as in the 20th century, namely the creation of a free organization of independent states which would eliminate wars and armed conflicts in general, outlaw any aggression, and maintain lasting world peace.

Another decisive factor which contributed to the new concept of an international community of independent states was undoubtedly the action taken by the Pope after the abrogation of the *Compactata* in organizing a large anti-Turkish campaign, for which he had won the support of the Duke of Burgundy, Venice and the King of Hungary.[16] If the King of Bohemia wanted to preserve his diplomatic initiative and effectively continue his struggle with the Holy See, into which he had been drawn against his will, he had to replace the planned anti-Turkish league and campaign by a new plan with a somewhat different and generally acceptable central point.

This new central point was the idea of a universal peace organization ensuring the peaceful settlement of international conflicts and constituting a generally recognized supranational authority of a thus far unknown type.

The new project was in full, inner conformity with the subsidiary action calling for a reform of the Holy Roman Empire, which had developed in close connection with the person of King George almost at the same time,[17] i.e. in 1463. The fact that a major role in this move, under which the reform was to be carried out by a treaty between the leading German princes, was played by Martin Mair, leads to the assumption that this outstanding German diplomat, politician and lawyer may also have been involved in the drafting of the projects of a universal peace organization which had just been initiated by King George. However, the two projects were not coordinated in detail. For example, it is remarkable that under the plan of the imperial reform, the Imperial Diet was to convene in Cheb (Eger) on the same Sunday *Reminiscere* (February 26, 1464) as envisaged in

---

15] *Ibid.*, p. 573. — Other circumstances which support the assumption that the final version of the project originated in Prague in the autumn of 1462 are listed by Urbánek, *op. cit.*, p. 591. — If I understand him correctly, the same assumption is favoured also by J. POLIŠENSKÝ, *Acta Universitatis Palackianae Olomucensis, Historica I*, 1960, p. 117.

16] Correctly noted by PALACKÝ, *op. cit.*, IV (ed. B. RIEGER), p. 410.

17] See PALACKÝ, *op. cit.*, pp. 417 *seq.* — R. URBÁNEK, *op. cit.*, 1962, pp. 332 *seq.*, and, pp. 677 *seq.*, particularly pp. 680 *seq.*

the grand project for the date of the constituent congress of the all-Christian peace organization in Basle.[18]

In the winter of 1462 to 1463, Marini again travelled through Europe,[19] apparently in an endeavour to pave the way at the various courts for the new and broader plan, although we do not know whether at that particular time he presented the whole project anywhere. By then the Pope had already received the first reports on the broad and, for many rulers, very attractive plan that had been conceived in Bohemia, which, however, was quite unacceptable from the viewpoint of the papal policy. Neither do we know to what extent the project, as we know it in its Polish version (summer 1463), had then been completed in written form.

Marini's mission at these diplomatic negotiations, whose course it is extremely difficult to reconstruct, was especially delicate at that time. His task was to prepare the ground for that "unbelievably bold political chess move",[20] which, as we may suspect from certain indications, he no longer fully supported. Apparently he well realized just what far-reaching proposals were involved and how profoundly their realization might change the existing political set-up of Europe and, in fact, of the whole, then known world. He knew that he could not produce the whole plan immediately anywhere, but rather that the best tactic he could use was simply to win, for the time being, support for the idea of general peace among the Christians, to be secured by a treaty which would be concluded at a congress of Christian rulers, and of common defence against the Turks. At the same time, he had to assure everybody that "the honour of the Holy Mother Church" etc. — as cited in the above-quoted principal directive of King George himself — would be preserved. Quite naturally, he also had to win approval specifically of the idea of a general treaty, proposed by King George, and speak very cautiously, or as little as possible, of the supranational body which would thus be formed and of its detailed organization. He could not divulge too much in advance because he was certainly too well aware of the fact that the Holy See was waiting for the first opportunity to accuse King George of preparing plans of a heretic nature.

At that time the conditions existing in Central Europe seemed favourable for the grand project.[21] Late in the autumn of 1462, King George had especially friendly relations with the Emperor, and the German princes turned to the Czech king — in spite of his strained relations with the Pope — with profound confidence and with great hopes that he would settle peacefully their disputes and contribute decisively not only to securing peace in Central Europe, but also to the proposed reform of the Holy Roman Empire. Moreover, the Czech crown had the most cordial relations with Poland, its relations with Hungary, whose youthful king was King George's son-in-law, also being satisfactory.

18] F. M. BARTOŠ, "Návrh krále Jiřího na utvoření svazu evropských států" (King George's Proposal for a Union of European States), *Jihočeský sborník historický* (South Bohemian Historical Annals), XII, 1939, p. 5. The author notes that according to the calendar then currently used in France, the date would have been March 10, 1465.

19] See URBÁNEK, *op. cit.*, 1962, pp. 592 and 642.

20] See *supra* p. 16.

21] The sceptical view expressed by R. HECK, *op. cit.*, p. 181, does not seem to be justified in this respect.

We cannot, of course, draw any conclusions which would lay claim to finality and universal recognition. Unless new facts are brought to light through an analysis of existing sources or the finding of thus far unknown sources, we can only offer a hypothesis. The key question is undoubtedly how it happened that Marini's proposals, which were still contained in his memorandum of 1462, were replaced at the end of the same year by a project which is documented in writing *in extenso* for the first time in the archives of the Polish Royal Chancellery in the summer of 1463. The most probable hypothesis, which we have explained above, is that in the autumn months of 1462 a project was conceived at the court of King George, which made much use of what had thus far been prepared by A. Marini, but which was the co-operative effort of several authors under the personal direction, it would seem, of King George himself. There is no doubt that a legal expert participated in the effort. Of the possible authors we have already named Martin Mair, to whom special attention was called — following the views expressed by František Palacký — by F. M. Bartoš a quarter of a century ago.[22] The assumption that there were several co-authors also seems to be indicated by the fact that the project is not uniform in form and substance, and that it shows certain small discrepancies.

It is quite clearly untenable to identify the proposal for a universal peace organization, as we know it from the years 1463 and 1464, with Marini's original proposals from the years 1461 and 1462. These original proposals, as can be judged, were in some respects similar to what had been conceived some 150 years earlier by Marini's fellow-countryman Pierre Dubois,[23] but, on the other hand, we have no evidence showing that Marini had read the writings of his predecessor or had become acquainted with them from any other source. King George's project constitutes such a departure from the various peace proposals dating from earlier times that we can hardly speak of any common features.[24]

Instead of vague, inconsistent, very primitive and, moreover, quite private considerations, the project whose 500th anniversary we are marking includes an extremely well worked-out system of rules governing interstate relations; it offers a picture of a new, supranational organization which is lucid in all its main points, was drawn up in the form of an official document worded in legal terms, and was discussed by the leading European powers of those days.

The historical reality which we have begun to discover in recent years was more complicated than we formerly believed. The diplomatic negotiations which Marini — serving King George — held at the various European courts between 1461 and 1464 apparently had two stages which fully

22] F. M. BARTOŠ, *op. cit.*, especially pp. 7 *seq.* (quoted from an extract). Bartoš's views are contested, but not convincingly, by R. URBÁNEK, *op. cit.*, 1962, especially on pp. 580 *seq.* Bartoš was also the first author to try (on pp. 5—6) to explain in detail the view already held by some authors, that King George's project, differing from Marini's original plans, was conceived in the autumn of 1462.

23] Compare with J. TER MEULEN, *op. cit.*, 1917, pp. 101 *seq.* — M. R. VESNITCH, "Deux précurseurs français du pacifisme" (P. Dubois et E. Crucé), Paris, 1911, *Extrait de la Révue d'histoire diplomatique*, pp. 1—60; E. ZECK, "Der Publizist Pierre Dubois", 1911; R. REDSLOB, "Das Problem des Völkerrechts", 1917, pp. 105 *seq.*; W. S. M. KNIGHT," The Mediaeval Pacifist Pierre Du Bois", *Transactions of the Grotius Society*, IX, 1924, I ; H. KÄMPF, *Pierre Dubois und die geistigen Grundlagen des französischen Nationalbewusstseins um 1300*, 1935.

24] See R. GILBERT, "Lulio y Vivez sobre la paz", in *La Paix*, II, Bruxelles 1961, pp. 125 *seq.*

conform to the two stages of the inner development of the project, as indicated at the beginning of this chapter.

In the first stage King George gave Marini full freedom to explore the possibility of establishing an alliance of the major Christian powers against the Turks. The alliance was to be formed at a congress of European rulers, was not to affect either the then Holy Roman Empire as a universal Christian monarchy, or the status of the Emperor and the Pope as the two heads of Christendom, and was to be upheld by the establishment of an international court of arbitration (known as a parliament), whose detailed organization was not determined.

In the second stage, which probably began in the autumn of 1462, the picture was quite different. The anti-Turkish crusade was moved to a secondary position and replaced by the principal objective of securing world peace. At this stage, Marini's and Dubois's princely court of arbitration became — under the name *consistorium* or *parlamentum* — one of the details, although an important one, of an ingeniously conceived, new international organism. The then existing organization of Christendom, headed by the Emperor and the Pope, was abandoned and replaced by a thus far unknown concept of a permanent union of independent and equal states in which there was no longer any place for the privileged status of the Emperor and the Pope.

King George's project is pictured in contemporary historical sources, insofar as they have been used for historical research, rather vaguely. This is especially obvious if we try to confront the substance of the project with the reports — mostly fragmentary — on the diplomatic negotiations held on the Prague proposals in various countries between 1462 and 1464. With only a few exceptions, which we shall list, such reports contain no detailed information on what we appreciate most in King George's project and for which we are marking its 500th anniversary, namely the new principles which were to govern the relations between individual states, and, to some extent, their internal affairs as well; neither do these reports provide much information on the revolutionary changes which the project, had it been realized, would have caused in the organization of Europe.

Thus, the Venetian reports[1] on Marini's talks with the French king in the winter of 1462—1463 mention most superficially certain proposals *quae honorem dei fideique defensionem concernant*, and indicate only very indistinctly that the subject of the negotiations in France was a *confederation* which the King of France was to conclude with the King of Bohemia *et aliis regibus et potentatibus colligatis*. Once again the reports lay stress on the merger of all Christian armed forces against the Turks as the principal aim of the negotiations; this moment is especially prominent in the letters sent by the Venetian leaders to the Kings of Bohemia, Poland and Hungary.[2] The message sent in this connection by the King of France to the King of Poland on January 28, 1463,[3] also contains nothing which would point in greater detail to the substance of the project as delivered from the King of Bohemia to the King of Poland by Marini himself in the summer of that same year. We come to the same conclusion if we analyze the reports which the Pope received early in

1]   PALACKÝ, *Urkundliche Beiträge*, 1860, p. 290.

2]   *Ibid.*, pp. 291—292.

3]   Compare R. HECK, *op. cit.*, p. 176.

1463 on Marini's negotiations in France and other countries, if, of course, we can rely on how these reports were reproduced for the Court at Milan.[4]

It is rather surprising to read a report contained in an almost identical version in a letter the Venetians[5] had sent to King Louis XI in March, 1463, and in the reply Marini received in Buda[6] a year later; the report states that in the winter of 1462—1463, the French king was willing to join some sort of a European league only if Marini was furnished with the proper mandate:

VENICE 1463

...*quod si idem orator and hoc mandatum habuisset, libenter cum*, ...*rege Bohemiae at aliis regibus et potentatibus colligatis ad confederationem devenisset (sc. rex Franciae)*...[7]

BUDA 1464

...*quid praefatus christianissimus Francorum rex, si modo vos de pleno mandato decuissetis, statim ad omnia paratus exstitisset et ligam generalem cum principibus Christianis sine dilatione iniisset.*[7]

From the legal point of view it is rather difficult to imagine the wording of such a document. The new and unprecedented political body which was at the core of King George's proposals could not come into existence in any other way than by a multilateral treaty drawn up and approved at a congress of those who were to be its first members. At the most, there could have been a letter authorizing the bearer to conclude an agreement between the Czech and the French kings (and perhaps other rulers) that they would convene such a congress.

In this connection we must also take note of the questions posed to the joint Czech, Polish and Hungarian mission by the French court officials during the negotiations of 1464, as regards the mandate of the mission. Some authors hold the view that at that time Albrecht Kostka of Postupice and Antonius Marini were furnished with a special mandate, but only for King Louis XI, to whom they personally submitted it.[8] I believe that this is not the only possible explanation. The Diary of the mission expressly notes Marini's reply to the French dignitaries "that at this time of the present embassy we required no longer documentary commission".[9] I understand this to

---

4] L. Pastor, *Geschichte der Päpste im Zeitalter der Renaissance*, 10th—12th editions, 1928, pp. 736—737, No. 57.

5] See footnote No. 1.

6] S. Katona, *Historia critica regum Hungariae*, t. VII (14), 1792, p. 705.

7] Translations: "... if the self-same ambassador had possessed the mandate therefore, he (the King of France) would have gladly concluded ... with the King of Bohemia and other allied kings and rulers a contractual confederation ..." (Venice, 1463); "... that the said Most Christian King of France, if you had only presented him with your mandate, would have immediately been willing to agree to everything and would have instituted without delay a general league with all the Christian princes". (Buda, 1464)

8] R. Urbánek, *op. cit.*, IV, 1962, p. 761, footnote No. 247.

9] *Archiv Český*, VII, p. 436; A. H. Wratislaw, *Diary of an Embassy from King George of Bohemia to King Louis XI of France*, London 1871, p. 40. The Czech term *poručenie listovnie* means the same as *litterae commissoriae* or *mandatum in scriptis*.

mean that the mission did not in fact have any other mandate than that permitting them to negotiate with the French king the convening of a congress of rulers (or their delegates) to which the project would be submitted.

The first document showing that at its time the project was understood in its true sense and in its consequences, is the heading with which the project was furnished when its text was transcribed into the *Metryka koronna* in summer, 1463, by a scribe of the Polish Royal Chancellery. The project was characterized correctly as *Tractatus pacis toti christianitati fiendae*,[10] which is a very general characterization but also a very telling one. The German report (intended for Prussia) on the deliberations at the Diet at Piotrków, which opened in October, 1463, mentions the project approximately in the same terms as the reply Marini received in Buda in March, 1464, and as the already mentioned Diary of the Czech mission to France. It lays primary stress on the constituent assembly of rulers, or their representatives, which was to establish the universal peace organization. Special attention is paid to the position of the Emperor and the Pope.[11]

The historical sources contain certain references only to the final stages of the negotiations concerned with the project, which indicate that statesmen and diplomats in Hungary and in France began to realize with some measure of surprise and awe just how revolutionary and novel the ideas contained in King George's proposals actually were.

The records of the discussions held in the Hungarian royal council between the end of March and late April 1464 contain a reproach addressed to the Czech king, in which he is accused of failing to notify his son-in-law, the King of Hungary, in advance when such serious matters were undertaken in his name:

et merito exspectasset sua serenitas a domino rege Bohemiae prius condignam superinde avisationem quam talia suo nomine fuissent mota et incepta.[12]

The political body which was to be established under the project was characterized in this document as *liga generalis*. It was correctly understood as being designed to secure *universalis inter christianos concordia*, and that all Christian states associated in this body were to be *in unum corpus redigi et ad celerem ac firmam concordiam deduci.*

The Hungarian document stressed further that this was the only proper way (*via*), *per quam in commune bonum omnia dirigerentur.* It is interesting that the word *pax* was not used in this

---

10] See *supra*, p. 31.

11] Compare R. HECK, *op. cit.*, p. 176. M. TOEPPEN, *Acten der Ständetage Preussens unter der Herrschaft des Deutschen Ordens,* V, Leipzig, 1886, No. 35, pp. 83—84. This extremely interesting report, too, has not yet been fully analyzed and properly exploited. It certainly merits much greater attention by scholars both as regards the *origin* of the project and its *interpretation* (the relationship of the new organization to the Pope and the Emperor, the question of its finances, etc.).

12] KANTONA, *op. cit.*, p. 706. — Compare with URBÁNEK, *op. cit.*, 1962, pp. 753—754, where, however, only little use is made of this source. A very good reproduction (in Czech) of the reply given to Marini by the Hungarian Royal Council is contained in PALACKÝ, *op. cit.*, IV, pp. 424—425. — Translation of the quoted passage: "and His Serenity would have rightly expected from the King of Bohemia proper and advance notification before *such important matters* were initiated in His name".

Hungarian characteristic of King George's proposals, although — as we have seen — it is the central term on which the project was built up. King George was reproached in a polemic tone for not paying enough attention to the war against the Turks, whose brunt was allegedly borne for all Christendom mostly by Hungary.

A direct reaction to the project is a passage which recapitulates the proposal to establish a universal peace organization as follows:

> *Cuius quidem ligae etiam capitalia quaedam puncta praesentastis, in quibus inter alia continetur de oratoribus regum et principum cum amplissima facultate ad certum locum et tempus destinandis qui rerum omnium omnimodam potestatem habeant et de occurrentibus quibuslibet pro communi utilitate disponant.*[13]

The scope of the jurisdiction of the general assembly, or the permanent congress of delegates (*congregatio*), as proposed in the project, is well expressed in the above passage, although, as its opening words indicate, Marini even then did not deem it propitious to present the whole text of the project at the Hungarian court.

As regards the final negotiations in France late in June and early in July, 1464, we are surprised to read in the Czech mission's Diary the reply given at the first, solemn audience by King Louis XI (who had, of course, previously held special talks with Marini). After all the negotiations that had taken place in the preceding years, the French king suddenly said that "this matter and desire of the King of Bohemia (namely that the King of France convene the constituent congress of the universal peace organization) was a great matter and that it was not meet to give an answer thereto so soon, but with good consideration".[14]

These facts we have just brought up, using quotes from historical sources, raise a number of questions. All those who took part in the diplomatic negotiations had apparently not all been informed in the same manner and therefore did not understand equally well the substance of the project. It seems that some of them were left too long at that stage of information — evolved from Marini's initial diplomatic missions — when the subject of the negotiations was simply the establishment of an anti-Turkish league of European rulers and of an associated court of justice — a parliament.

We must first ask whether King George's project was always presented in the full, final version from the years 1462 and 1463 to all those with whom it was discussed.[15] Thus far we know for certain that the full text was submitted only to the King of Poland and that the main points of the project (*capitalia quaedum puncta*) were communicated to the King of Hungary.

We must also ask whether the respective rulers and their court officials and dignitaries, with

13] Translation: "You also submitted some principal points of this league, which provide, among other things, that the ambassadors of the kings and princes, furnished with the fullest of powers, should meet at a certain place and at a certain time, who would have all-round competence over all matters and would decide for the common good on all matters that might occur."

14] *Archiv Český*, VII, p. 436; WRATISLAW, *Diary*, p. 37.

15] For different opinion expressed in this respect in existing literature see R. HECK, *op. cit.*, p. 168, footnote No. 46.

whom the matter was discussed, devoted due attention to the proposals and, in particular, whether they analyzed and understood them correctly. It seems that also in this respect the situation varied greatly at the various courts.

Finally, we cannot but ask to what extent the reports that have been preserved on the project were affected by the fact that Marini's talks with the responsible officials in the individual states were in most cases extremely confidential, and even secret,[16] so that they were not usually recorded in writing, or at least not in those sources that have been preserved.

The reports we have on the project must therefore be evaluated in connection with all that has just been indicated. The fact that especially the circumstances noted in the last question played an important role is shown by the notes contained on the project in the Diary of the mission dispatched from Prague to France in May, 1464. They indicate that except for the two leading members of the mission, Lord Albrecht Kostka of Postupice and Antonius Marini, none of the other members of the mission knew the detailed provisions of the project. They knew only that the mission was to ask the King of France, on behalf of the Czech, Polish and Hungarian kings, to convene "a parliament and convocation of Christian kings and princes",[17] while some minor details, identical with the wording of the Charter, are contained in the transcript of the speech made by the leader of the mission to the King of France.[18] However, the Diary conforms fully to the contents of the project in that it does not contain even the slightest hint of an anti-Turkish campaign or, in general, of the assumed anti-Turkish aim of this great diplomatic move.

The same conclusions may be drawn from the reports on the Czech mission to Louis XI sent from France to Italy by the ambassadors of Milan.[19] Only the panicky reaction which the project evoked in the procurator of the city of Wrocław (Breslau) in Rome in the late summer of 1464 indicates that the enemies of King George had acquainted themselves with the proposed Charter and had studied it with fanatic hate. However, we shall discuss this point in Chapter 8.[20]

Moreover, all those passages in the Diary of the mission which describe the course of the negotiations in France and, in particular, the most cautious and strictly confidential talks between the Czech ambassadors and the King of France and his highest aides[21] before the ceremonial audience and afterwards confirm that this is how we should proceed in explaining many of those things which we have hitherto failed to grasp in studying the preserved reports concerning King George's project.

However, the events which we have touched upon in this connection are the subject of the next chapter.

16] See URBÁNEK, *op. cit.* 1962, p. 761, footnote No. 247; R. HECK, *op. cit.*, p. 178.

17] *Archiv Český*, VII, p. 436, compare with p. 437.

18] See *infra* on p. 54.

19] B. de MANDROT, *Dépêches des ambassadeurs milanais en France sous Louis XI. et François Sforza*, II, Paris, 1919, pp. 206—208.

20] See *infra* on p. 58—59.

21] *Archiv Český*, VII, pp. 436—438; WRATISLAW, *Diary*, pp. 38—44. — Also compare *infra* on p. 55—56.

The Sunday *Reminiscere* (February 26) of 1464, when the congress of Christian rulers was to have met in Basle to establish the universal peace organization proposed by King George, passed without the preparatory talks having been concluded. King George and King Casimir of Poland had already agreed on a joint procedure in this matter,[1] but the royal court in Prague deemed it essential that the project should be supported by yet another, third sponsor, King Matthias of Hungary, whose position had not yet been ascertained. It could be assumed from previous negotiations that the Hungarian court would approve the plan of an anti-Turkish league, as originally proposed by Marini, and that it would have especially welcomed a large-scale military campaign against the Turks in the Balkans, but it was precisely these points which receded into the background in King George's new project to give way to other proposals which were far less attractive to Hungary in view of the current international situation.

Antonius Marini arrived in Buda for more negotiations only several weeks after the unfortunate death in childbirth of King Matthias' young wife Kunhuta, who was King George's daughter, who had been an important personal link between the two rulers. Marini's mission turned out to be not exactly favourable. There seems to be doubt that Marini strictly followed King George's instructions to divulge only the essentials of the prepared text of the grand project, but even this precaution did not fully protect him from the danger that he would be declared a heretic by the Hungarian church hierarchy because of the cause he promoted.[2] The papal party was too powerful in Hungary not to have influenced the final reply Marini received from the whole of the royal council in April.

The text of this reply, which represents one of the most important documents in the history

---

1]   These questions have now been explained by R. HECK, *op. cit.*, in particular on pp. 177 *seq.*

2]   According to the report in the Diary, Marini told Louis XI right at the first solemn audience, how in Hungary "some bishops wished to excommunicate him", *Archiv Český* VII, p. 435; WRATISLAV, *Diary*, p. 36.

of King George's peace proposals, has been preserved[3] and has been quoted several times in the present study. The organization of Christian states, proposed by King George, is defined as *liga generalis* or as *universalis concordia*, which is a very expressive term. The reply also states that Marini had submitted to the Hungarian Court *capitalia quaedam puncta*, that is, not the whole project drawn up in Prague, and the Czech king was reproached for not having informed the Hungarian royal court well in advance and in full of such an important matter. This reproach appears twice in the Hungarian reply, and today we can hardly doubt its validity or suspect King Matthias of having denied some previous negotiations on this subject.[4]

It is indeed most probable that such proposals were not discussed with the King of Hungary, and the Hungarian reply says just that. *Ceterum ista huiusmodi universalis concordiae et generalis ligae mentio hic apud maiestatem regiam fuit hactenus inaudita*, notes the Hungarian document, and adds in another place: *Sed, quia, ut praedictum est, apud regiam maiestatem usque ad hoc tempus haec fuerunt inaudita ...*

King Matthias did not reject the submitted proposals in principle and actually praised their noble aim,[5] reserving, however, the right to notify his allies against the Turks, i.e. the Venetians, and, in particular, the Emperor and the Pope:

> *eos, cum quibus aliquam intelligentiam habet, ut Venetos, et praesertim principalissima totius christianitatis capita, sedem videlicet apostolicam et imperatoriam celsitudinem, priusquam ad specialiores conclusiones descensus fiat, super his aliquantulum reddere certiores.*[6]

However, King Matthias did not finally veto King George's proposals, but, on the contrary, gave Marini the mandate to convey also on his behalf (for Marini already had a similar mandate from King Casimir) to King Louis XI the wish that a general congress of Christian rulers be convened over which the French king would preside.

The result was a very complex situation which historians have not yet succeeded in elucidating properly. A far-reaching project of a new organization of human society had been drawn up which had not yet been either accepted or rejected *in merito*. It was to be discussed at a congress of Christian rulers, which was to be convened by King Louis XI of France. King George of Bohemia, King Casimir of Poland and King Matthias of Hungary — the last with certain reservations — merely agreed that they would jointly ask the French king to convene the congress.

3] It was published by S. KATONA in Vol. VII (14) of his *Historia critica regum Hungariae stirpis mixtae*, 1792, pp. 704 *seq.* See also *supra*, p. 47.

4] This was still done by R. URBÁNEK, *op. cit.*, 1962, p. 753.

5] *Nihil optabilius, nihil melius, nihil salutarius contingere posset populis christianis ...* (Translation "The Christian nations could receive nothing they could desire more, nothing better and nothing more beneficial ...")

6] Translation: "to give at least some notice to those with whom he has an agreement, such as the Venetians, and especially to the principal heads of all Christendom, namely the Apostolic See and His Imperial Highness, *before more specific conclusions have been reached*".

We have learned of other important events concerning the project from a unique historical source, viz. the most intelligently and amusingly, even if too briefly written "Diary of an Embassy from King George of Bohemia to the King of France"[7] discovered by František Palacký in 1826 and published by him for the first time in 1827. The Diary was written in Czech by a member of the mission — most probably by the page Jaroslav — and its frankness, attractive descriptions and authenticity make it one of the most interesting Czech literary documents of the late Middle Ages. The report of the Diary on the course of negotiations at the Court of King Louis XI of France has never been analyzed from the viewpoint of diplomatic history. Therefore, this unique historical source has not yet been fully exploited for the drawing of a clear picture of the last stage of the struggle for realization of King George's great project. It is possible, of course, that a study of the French archives — which has also yet to be made — will supplement the Diary in some respects.

On May 16, 1464, a mission of 30 to 40 horsemen left Prague for the purpose of persuading the King of France to convene a congress of Christian rulers which would establish a universal peace organization. Besides this main task, the mission was also instructed to try to obtain in any form whatsoever the conclusion of a treaty of friendship between the Czech and the French kings. Both objectives were of the utmost importance for King George, although it is quite clear that the first aim represented the main task of the mission, the attainment of the second being only of secondary importance.

In view of the struggle between the Roman Church and the King of Bohemia, the convening of a general congress of Christian rulers would have demonstrated to the whole world that the Pope rather than King George stood in political isolation. In any case, however, the conclusion of a treaty of friendship between the Czech king and "the Most Christian King" would have shown that King George, whom the Pope had declared a heretic, was not as isolated as the Pope would have wished him to be. At that time the King of Bohemia did indeed face the danger of certain isolation in international politics especially in connection with the failure of the already mentioned plans for the reform of the Holy Roman Empire, which had still looked so promising in the winter of 1462 to 1463.

For the purpose of its main task, the mission was furnished with credentials (*litterae credentiales*) both from the King of Bohemia and the Kings of Poland and Hungary. The head of the mission was the Czech nobleman Albrecht (Albert) Kostka of Postupice, who represented the King of Bohemia. Second in order was Chevalier Antonius Marini, who acted on behalf of King Casimir of Poland and King Matthias of Hungary. In addition, Albrecht Kostka was furnished with a

7] The best edition was prepared by Josef KALOUSEK in *Archiv Český*, VII, Prague, 1887, pp. 427—445. — Out of date is the edition of F. PALACKÝ in *Časopis Společnosti wlastenského Museum v Čechách* (Journal of the Society of the National Museum in Bohemia), II/1, 1827, pp. 40—67. Nevertheless, a good English translation of this first edition was prepared by A. H. WRATISLAW under the title *Diary of an Embassy from King George of Bohemia to King Louis XI of France in the Year of Grace 1464*, London, 1871, pp. 1—80. — A German extract from Palacký's edition of the Diary was published in the *Monatschrift der Gesellschaft des böhmischen Museums*, Prague 1827, pp. 44—59. — Another edition was prepared by R. URBÁNEK in the book *Ve službách Jiříka krále. Deníky panoše Jaroslava a Václava Šaška z Bířkova* (In the Service of King George. Diaries of Page Jaroslav and of Václav Šašek of Bířkov), Prague, 1940, pp. XLVII + 220.

special mandate (*litterae commissoriae*) from the King of Bohemia to conclude the Czecho-French treaty of friendship. As regards other mandates and full powers, this question, on which we have already touched,[8] still remains unsolved.

The journey of the mission took it through Bayreuth, Nuremberg, Stuttgart, Baden, Strassbourg, Toul, Reims and Amiens, because in France the messengers learned that King Louis XI was hunting in northwestern France. By the end of June the mission caught up with the king near Abbeville on the borderline between Picardy and Normandy.

After three preliminary, unofficial and private talks on June 22, 28 and 30, between Louis XI and Marini alone — we should remember that he was also a counsellor of the French king — the mission as a whole was received on the afternoon of Saturday, June 30, by the king in a solemn audience held in the presence of the king's council in a "castle in the midst of marshes" whose name the author of the Diary noted as "Dumpiir" (today undoubtedly Dompierre).

However, let us hear from the author himself, who described the course of the audience not only authentically but also in a most colourful and vivid manner.[9]

When we were admitted into the presence of His Majesty, Lord Albert Kostka first pronounced a formal salutation from the King of Bohemia and forthwith delivered the letter credential from the self-same King of Bohemia. Then Lord Antony likewise pronounced a salutation from the Kings of Hungary and Poland, and forthwith delivered letters credential from both Kings. Then the King himself read the letters credential to his council, but he read that of the King of Bohemia first. And when he had read them all through, he bade Lord Kostka and Lord Antony take their places upon a seat prepared for the purpose. They declined and refused to sit down till the King's council said that it was customary for royal ambassadors to perform their embassy sitting. And before they took their seats two members of the council, coming up to Lord Kostka and Lord Antony, told them from the King that His Majesty wished us to perform our embassy as briefly as possible and to speak briefly. Then Lord Kostka said that he would speak briefly, and so they sat down and spoke.

First, Lord Albert Kostka spoke in Latin, excusing himself and saying that he had rather perform the duties of a knight than speak in the presence of so mighty and Most Christian King; and thus he spoke long and much, all of which I could not write down here word for word. But, briefly, the end and intent of all this speech was this: that the King of Bohemia entreated and prayed the King of France, as the Most Christian King, and one who loved the common good of the Christian faith, that His Majesty would be pleased to bring to pass a parliament and convocation of Christian kings and princes, to meet in person or by their plenipotentiaries in one place and at one time, where and when the King of France should appoint and ordain; and that the King of

8]   See p. 47.

9]   *Archiv Český*, VII, pp. 435—436; Wratislaw, *Diary*, pp. 37—38.

Bohemia desired this for the glory of God and the exaltation of the Christian Faith and of the Holy Roman Catholic Church, and for the Holy Christian Empire, etc. And this he expressed at good breadth and length, so that it took about an hour or more. Likewise also Lord Antony spoke on the same matter, in Latin from the King of Poland and in French from the King of Hungary, although he said from both Kings more than Lord Kostka had expressed from the King of Bohemia. For he spoke, recounting what had happened to him at the court of the King of Hungary, how some bishops had wished to excommunicate him, and what he had heard there concerning the King of France, how the Pope had written letters reviling His Majesty; likewise also concerning the adventures, which he had met with at the court of the King of Poland; and likewise he related what had happened to him, when he went from the King of France to the Venetian lords; and how lovingly disposed the King of Bohemia, the King of Poland and the King of Hungary were towards the King of France, and how greatly their subjects loved the King of France; and especially that the Bohemian lords were very well inclined towards the King and Kingdom of France, and so likewise were the Venetian lords. And all this he expressed very fully in Latin and in French.

Thereto the King of France commanded answer to be made through his chancellor, that this matter and desire of the King of Bohemia, which Lord Albert Kostka had stated, was a great matter, and that it was not meet to give an answer thereto so soon, but with good consideration. So he commanded, that we should go back again to Abbeville, and promised that the King would follow us on Tuesday, or at latest on Wednesday, forthwith, and that then he would make an end and settlement for us concerning all matters.

The mission remained in the vicinity of the French king for more than two weeks, but the negotiations did not reach a further, more favourable stage regarding the proposals made by the Czech, Polish and Hungarian kings. The postponement requested by the French king was used by the papal party at his court to foil the acceptance of the proposal to convene a congress of Christian rulers. As we learn from the Diary,[10] they received support in this respect directly from Bohemia, from where opponents of King George had sent letters to the French king warning him that George was a heretic. Louis XI needed an ally against the powerful French feudal lords and especially against Burgundy, but, on the other hand, he was afraid that a close and open alliance with George, especially through the acceptance of the proposals for convening a congress of Christian rulers, would turn against him not only the Pope, but also the French prelates who might have openly joined his enemies.

On July 11, Marini held another private talk with Louis XI, and presumably — the Diary laeves us in doubt in this respect — Albrecht Kostka held a secret talk with the French king on July 13 (?). In any case, we may agree with Urbánek that the Czech envoys did speak with the king in private, even though we do not know when.[11] It is most probable that Kostka used the occasion

10] *Ibid.*, p. 437; *Diary*, pp. 43—44. See URBÁNEK, *op. cit.*, 1962, p. 760.

11] URBÁNEK, *op. cit.*, 1962, p. 757, footnote No. 237; also p. 758.

to present to the French king secret documents which he was instructed not to show to anybody else.[12]

Meanwhile, the leaders of the mission held conferences with leading French court officials on the proposals the mission had presented to the king on June 30. The reports in the Diary are laconic, but nevertheless they show who were the chief opponents of the proposals. Very dramatic was, in particular, the conversation between Albrecht Kostka and Marini on the one hand, and, on the other hand, between members of the French royal council some time in the second week of July. There was a sharp exchange of views in which the French prelates openly declared that the proposals presented by the Czech mission ran counter to the status, functions and authority of the Pope and the Emperor:

> that the King of Bohemia ought not to desire this, especially without the consent of the Holy Father, the Pope, and the Christian Emperor; and that it would appertain best to the Holy Father to negotiate this with the Emperor; and that the King of Bohemia ought not to interfere in the matter.[13]

The Czech envoys were also quite frank in their replies. Their statements condemning the Pope, the policy of the Catholic Church and the relationship between the Papal Curia and individual states were so pointed that when František Palacký published the Diary in 1827, he did not reproduce them in full in fear of the official Austrian censorship.[14]

Eventually, on July 15, another solemn audience was held, at which the leaders of the Czech mission met with the French king and his council. There is no mention anywhere of any discussion on the proposals which the mission had presented on June 30. There was probably no point in discussing them any further. However, at this second meeting King Louis XI decided to conclude without delay a treaty of friendship with the King of Bohemia, pointing out that it represented a restoration of old treaties; he did so — as Marini stressed, according to the Diary — in spite of objections raised by the bishops sitting in the royal council.[15] On that same day, the leader of the Czech mission, Albrecht Kostka of Postupice, was honoured by being appointed to membership in the French royal council. The members of the Czech mission then took formal leave of the king, although Marini had one more private conference with him on the Czecho-French treaty.

Thus the mission accomplished at least its smallest objective. Its main programme had failed so utterly that nothing more was heard of it in the subsequent period. Antonius Marini left the

---

12]   *Ibid.*, p. 760, footnote No. 247. — Compare *supra*, p. 50.

13]   *Archiv Český*, VII, p. 437.

14]   Compare the Palacký edition (see *supra* in footnote No. 7), p. 54, with the Kalousek edition, p. 437. Wratislaw's *Diary* does not contain the sharp condemnation of the Pope either. For Palacký's anxiety not to offend the Austrian censor see the editor's note in Kalousek, *ibid.*

15]   *Archiv Český*, VII, p. 438: "And Lord Antony said, that the King spoke in the council to those bishops and the rest, saying: 'Whether any one like it or mislike it, I will be on good terms with the King of Bohemia, and will enter into goodwill and friendship with him'. And forthwith he commanded his council to complete the letters ...". Wratislaw, *Diary*, pp. 47—48.

mission shortly after it had set out on its return home, never to return to the services of King George. The mission returned to Bohemia via Rouen, Paris, Orléans, Lyon, Geneva, Berne, Constance, Passau and České Budějovice. On September 14, 1464, it joined King George who was then staying in Brno.

In the meantime, the conflict between King George and the Pope had gained in intensity; exactly one month after the mission had left Prague, Pope Pius II summoned the Czech king to appear before the papal court within 180 days to stand accused of a number of the most serious crimes, including heresy. We should add that King George, quite naturally, never went to Rome. When two years later, under the reign of the next pope, Paul II, he was sentenced *in absentia*, proclaimed a "son of perdition", a heretic and perjurer, and stripped of his royal title, King George appealed to the General Council and continued to rule in Bohemia, this state of affairs prevailing until his death in 1471.

HISTORIANS AND LAWYERS DISCOVER THE 15th
CENTURY PEACE PROJECT

There are written documents concerning the peace project of King George in all the countries where diplomatic negotiations on the peace-making league of Christian states were held between 1462 and 1464, these documents naturally differing in their contents and historical value. We have already mentioned a number of them in our endeavour to draw a correct picture of the origin of the project and in tracing the response with which the project met at its time.

Surprisingly enough, not a single manuscript of the project has yet been found in Bohemia, although practically all the diplomatic negotiations emanated from the court of King George. On the other hand, one of the most valuable documents concerning the whole matter — the Diary of the Czech mission to King Louis XI of France in 1464, written in Czech[1] — had been preserved in Bohemia until the 19th century when, following its second publication, it got lost.

The full text of the project, as far as we know, exists in three countries:[2] in France, whose ruler was expected to become the head of the proposed supranational organization, in Poland, whose king was King George's closest ally in promoting the peace organization, and in Austria, then the seat of the Emperor. The recent discovery of the most valuable manuscript in Warsaw, which was used as the basis for the reconstruction of King George's project on pp. 00—00 of this anniversary publication, seems to indicate that there may still be other manuscripts awaiting discovery, especially in Italy, France and Germany.

It is quite interesting that the preservation of the text of King George's project for posterity was unwittingly due also to the zeal of the papal adherents in the European high diplomacy of King George's times. One of the king's enemies in Rome — the procurator of the city of Wrocław [Breslau], which was hostile to the Czech king — succeeded in the summer of 1464 in acquiring the

1]   See *supra* on p. 53.

2]   Information on the manuscripts according to the state existing before World War II was provided by F. M. BARTOŠ in the study quoted in detail *supra* on p. 43, footnote No. 18.

text of the project, allegedly — as he was assured — from a member of the French royal council. He had eight copies made and sent one of them directly to the Pope with a note saying that the document contained at least ten articles *die gantz wider die heiligen Kirchen sein*. In his zeal he also added a piece of information which must have come as a shock, but which was quite erroneous, namely that the document was a secret treaty concluded between the Most Christian King and the king of heretics (*copien der bünde und vorschreibung, die der könig Francie mit dem kätzer getan hat*). He also sent a similar report to his masters in Wrocław. The conclusions drawn by F. M. Bartoš[3] in connection with this source may be considered correct.

Almost 300 years elapsed before the text of the project was published in print, while the publication of the Diary took even longer. When eventually both documents became accessible to historians — the former in 1747, in Lenglet's edition of Commines' Mémoirs,[4] and the latter in 1827, in F. Palacký's edition[5] — several more decades passed before the mutual relationship of the two basic sources was analyzed.

Palacký, who, on the basis of the information contained in the Diary, confirmed by some other, fragmentary reports, quite correctly estimated the true purpose of the project and highly praised it, never suspected until the last years of his life that a text of the project might exist. Taillandier,[6] who wrote of King George's plans with the utmost sympathy in 1862, also could not base his thesis on an analysis of the actual text and consequently his arguments were not sufficiently convincing.

Thus the first scientific analysis of King George's project was undertaken as late as in 1869 by the Silesian historian H. Markgraf,[7] who in his study brilliantly applied the methods of the German historiography of the second half of the 19th century, but did not show much understanding of the actual purpose and historical significance of King George's proposals. He viewed the project as a historic curiosity, regarding it primarily as a plan for the creation of an anti-Turkish league, which view has influenced a section of historiography right up to today. Markgraf expressly defined the peace-making aspect of the project as "fantastic and unrealizable",[8] which was in keeping with the intellectual atmosphere of Bismarck's Germany.

3] *Op. cit.*, p. 20. — He interprets a report dated September 29, 1464, *Scriptores rerum Silesiacarum*, IX, Breslau, 1874, p. 97, which we have already mentioned (p. 24). Although it does not mention expressly either King George or his proposal for a peace league, the report is quite clear in its hints. — The erroneous view that the project of a universal peace organization formed part of a Czecho-French treaty concluded in July, 1464, can also be found in modern historical literature. See P. M. PERRET, *Histoire des relations de la France avec Venise*, I, Paris, 1896, p. 435.

4] LENGLET du FRESNOY (Dufrenoy), *Mémoires de Messire Philippe de Comines, seigneur d'Argenton*, Paris — Londres, 1747, II, Annex No. XXXVI, pp. 424 *seq*. This edition is probably based on a copy of the project rather than on its original text.

5] See *supra*, p. 39, footnote No. 8.

6] Saint-René TAILLANDIER, "Le roi George de Podiebrad, épisode de l'histoire de Bohême, II, La lutte du roi de Bohême et du Saint-Siège," *Revue des deux mondes*, vol. 40, 32/2, Paris, 1862, pp. 915—956.

7] H. MARKGRAF, "Über Georg's v. Podiebrad Project eines christlichen Fürstenbundes zur Vertreibung der Türken aus Europa und Herstellung des allgemeinen Friedens innerhalb der Christenheit", *Historische Zeitschrift*, vol. 21, 1869, pp. 245—304.

8] *Ibid.* p. 258. — Compare also with an evaluation dating from a more recent period: ". . . the whole scheme was too fantastic to be acceptable to Louis XI or to anybody else," A. NUSSBAUM, *A Concise History of the Law of Nations*, New York, 1947, p. 50.

It took one whole generation before some scholars began to pay attention to those values of the project for which it is now famous all over the world. 440 years after the project had been drafted, the ideas of King George and his advisors were re-discovered by historians of international law. In this respect we must be most grateful to the Czech professor of international law A. Zucker,[9] who called attention to King George's proposals in connection with the first Peace Conference at the Hague in 1899, and to W. Schücking, who shortly afterwards introduced King George's project into the world literature on international law and steered the study of the project onto the proper course.

In 1904, Schücking (referring to Palacký) reproached E. Nys for having made a serious error in completely omitting King George's project in the historical part of his French work, thereby substantially distorting the story of the peace efforts in Europe.[10] Four years later the same author underlined the significance of the project in his well-known treatise outlining the development of the legal organization of human society,[11] when earlier he had suggested to one of his students that he should write the first monograph — first from the viewpoint of legal history — on this topic whose political timeliness — seven years before the outbreak of World War I — was being increasingly felt.[12]

King George's project was then finally raised to a place of honour in the history of the peace movement and international organization by J. Ter Meulen[13] and Christian Lange.[14] This, however, happened at a time when it seemed that after 455 years King George's ideas would be realized in the League of Nations, established one year after the end of World War I. A search for parallels between the League of Nations Pact and King George's project was quite common in literature of legal history or international law in the period between the two world wars;[15] however, the authors did not always tackle these complex questions with a full knowledge of their historical connections.

In that same period, too, the historical parts of textbooks on international law always mentioned — some with a measure of accuracy, others superficially — King George of Poděbrady as the predecessor of the idea of the League of Nations.

9] A. ZUCKER, "Jiří Poděbradský a české mezinárodní styky v 15. století" (George of Poděbrady and Czech International Relations in the 15th Century), *Česká revue*, IV, 1901, p. 134. The author wanted to assess the historical significance of the project and its timeliness as well as to popularize the results of the first Peace Conference at the Hague in 1899.

10] *Zeitschrift für internationales Privat- und öffentliches Recht*, XIV, 1904, p. 554.

11] Walther SCHÜCKING, "Die Organisation der Welt" in *Festgabe für Paul Laband*, I, Tübingen, 1908, pp. 535—614, in particular pp. pp. 564—568.

12] Ernst SCHWITZKY, "Der europäische Fürstenbund Georg's von Podiebrad. Ein Beitrag zur Geschichte der Weltfriedensidee", *Arbeiten aus dem juristisch staatswissenschaftlichen Seminar*, No. 6, Marburg a. L. 1907.

13] Jacob TER MEULEN, *Der Gedanke der internationalen Organisation in seiner Entwicklung 1300—1800*, the Hague, 1917, pp. 108–123.

14] Christian L. LANGE, "Histoire de l'internationalisme, I", *Publications de l'Institut Nobel Norvégien*, No. 4, Oslo, 1919, pp. 112—113.

15] For more detailed information see V. VANĚČEK, "Eine Weltfriedensorganisation", *Sitzungsberichte der Deutschen Akademie*, Berlin, 1963, (cited fully *supra* on p. 11, footnote No 1), in particular p. 8.

When after World War II the United Nations Organization was founded, the primacy of its idea, too, was often ascribed to King George. An outstanding treatise on King George's project was written almost simultaneously with the adoption of the United Nations Charter by the Soviet legal historian V. M. Koretski,[16] who used the fitting title "The Project of George of Poděbrady to Establish an Organization of Peace and Security". The Soviet scholar made an attempt to describe the events of 1462—1464 in their European connections and to interpret King George's proposals as they had been conditioned by historical development without, however, lowering their epochal significance in any way. His work was also the first to analyze questions relating to the project from the Marxist point of view, which was very useful and instructive.

It is quite characteristic that only in the 20th century have we succeeded in fully grasping the true purpose, substance, core and aims of the proposals which originated in Prague 450 to 500 years ago. The central point of King George's project was the idea that lasting peace could be secured through a well-designed supranational organization which would outlaw the settlement of conflicts between individual states by means of war. The historical greatness not only of this idea itself, but also of the first attempt to realize it through official negotiations on the highest international level came to be fully appreciated only in a period when the principles contained in King George's project actually began to be put into effect. This is a classical example of the fact that mankind can fully understand and properly assess great ideas from its past only when it comes to see the beneficial effects of their realization in everyday practice.

16] Vladimir Mikhailovich KORETSKI, "Proyekt Yuriya Podiebrada ob organisatsii mira i bezopasnosti", *Izvestia Akademiyi Nauk SSSR, Otdel. ekonomiki i prava*, No. 5, 1946, pp. 382—396.

Although what we have said on the preceding pages may have sounded optimistic, we can hardly claim that we are fully satisfied with the current state of our knowledge concerning the peace proposals of King George. It is true that we know much more than in the days when the noted Czech historian Josef Šusta wrote his last report on Czech historical literature for the *Revue historique*, but the words Šusta used then, namely that the "mystery"[1] of this remarkable document was far from being solved, undoubtedly still hold true.

The main reason for this state of affairs seems to lie in the fact that the peace proposals of the "Hussite King" have thus far been studied by historians who were non-lawyers, or by lawyers — especially those concerned with international law — who lacked special training in historiography. The result has been that while in the sphere of international law the epochal significance of King George's project is readily recognized, historians, non-lawyers, often tend to view the project sceptically and even with certain distrust.

The second principal reason for our unsatisfactory knowledge about the peace league proposed by King George is the fact that until quite recently most of the works written on this topic were based on the text of a copy of rather doubtful origin published in a haphazard manner by Lenglet du Fresnoy in 1747. Thus, until 1939, researchers overlooked other texts, which are much more important and which we mentioned in the preceding chapter. It was only F. M. Bartoš[2] who pointed ed out that a much better source for analysis of the project was offered by those texts which opened (after the introductory "*In nomine Domini*") with the typical phrase "*Nos A B C notum facimus*" in contrast to the traditionally used text of Lenglet which opened with the phrase "*nos Georgius*,

---

1]   The French text of the report was never published in the *Revue historique* (Paris) because of the Munich events and the outbreak of World War II. As regards the Czech text, see Josef Šusta, *Posledních deset let československé práce dějepisné* (The Last Ten Years of Czechoslovak Historiography), Prague, 1937, p. 191.

2]   *Ibid.*, p. 12.

rex Bohemiae, notum facimus". The former group of texts, which includes also the most recently discovered text in Warsaw, shows especially well the character of the project as the outline of a multilateral international treaty, a fact of great significance for legal history. Just as in the case of any other historical work, a reliable, scientific analysis depends on an expert edition of the project, based on a comparative study of the greatest possible number of existing texts and otherwise in keeping with the scientific requirements of modern times.

Another thing that would be desirable is the presence in every country, in which the Czech proposals were discussed in the years 1462—1464, of a historian who would clarify on the basis of all available sources the role his country had played in the complex diplomatic negotiations. As a recent excellent example we may quote R. Heck, who has thoroughly explained in his often quoted study the Polish participation in the move initiated and led by King George. We would certainly know much more if a similar study of the negotiations on King George's project were made in Hungary, Italy,[3] and especially in France, which was the second centre of the political trends that found their expression in King George's project. Without the support of the French court, the project could probably have never been drafted.

A whole set of problems is raised by the question — considered objectively from the viewpoint of modern science — of the relationship between the proposals of King George and all that had preceded them in this respect in world history and, in particular, of what was done to prevent armed conflicts in Central Europe, where the project originated. Among other things, we shall have to study more thoroughly than hitherto the history of the term, concept and institution of *pax*, which forms the pivotal point of the whole project. We may assume that the authors of the project thought not only of international peace, but also of "peace" inside the individual countries, but there seems to be no doubt that the main stress was laid on peace in the international scope, as we have pointed out in Chapter 4.

A rather satisfactory analysis has already been made of the legal aspect of King George's project. The few existing shortcomings in this respect have been pointed out elsewhere.[4] In any case, we must always observe the basic rule that King George's proposals, viewed from the "legal aspect" — which must not be given precedence over the historical aspect or be forcibly separated from it — should not be given a different historical meaning than they actually have. What is needed is not a dogmatic legal analysis, which would approach the Charter from the same aspect as it does the existing law — but an analysis from the viewpoint of legal history. It would be especially useful to analyze the Charter according to the different spheres of law, for example, from the viewpoint of criminal law, of the history of administrative practices, and, of course, in particular from the viewpoint of the history of international law.

Of considerable importance, although it appears to be only a theoretical problem, but simultaneously one which seriously affects the overall approach to this historical phenomenon, is the

3] The description of the diplomatic negotiations held in Italy between 1462 and 1464, as contained in P. — M. PERRET, *Histoire des relations de la France avec Venise*, I, Paris, 1896, pp. 391 *seq.*, seems to be outdated.

4] *Sitzungsberichte*, 1963, p. 15.

question of whether we should view the project — as some authors do — as one of the many utopian ideas we find in history.[5] I believe that King George's project should not be placed among utopias in their true sense for the simple reason that it was never intended to bring about any comprehensive change in the contemporary social order; on the contrary, it was based rather on the social order which had developed in the individual countries in the course of history. At the time of the origin of the project, this could have been only the feudal order, especially if we bear in mind that the authors of the project were far from being social revolutionaries. The core of the whole matter lies in the fact that the project is based on principles which — as we can best see today — are applicable to relations between individual countries regardless of the respective social orders, as long as they enjoy full sovereignty. We should also bear in mind that the project formed part of a certain international, political campaign and was a living instrument of diplomatic negotiations.

Another problem still awaiting final solution is that of King George's aides. Thus far we know definitely only of Antonius Marini, whose name has been frequently mentioned in the present study. His participation in the project has been considerably overestimated in previous literature.[6] We must see that there is not yet a general recognition of the two stages of the origin of the project which we have tried to elucidate in detail in the present study and which have led us to conclude that Marini played a major role only in the first stage, when the principal ideas for which we remember the project today had not yet been formulated. An important, still unanswered question is that of the role played by M. Mair, and possibly other experts, in drawing up the project. Although Mair's participation is more than probable, it has not been proved in existing sources to such a degree that we might consider it indisputable.

King George's role, too, requires further study. The view is gradually being accepted that the king's role in the ideological authorship of the project was much greater than that of any of his aides, but once again this assumption is not sufficiently documented in the available sources of material.

The extent to which King George was a consistent opponent of the principle of settling international disputes by war is shown by the following characteristic incident: as late as one year before his death in 1470 King George proposed to the King of Hungary, who had meanwhile become his enemy, that they fight a personal duel should they fail to reach a peaceful settlement of their dispute. In truly mediaeval style he expressly offered King Matthias: "First peace, and if he should not want peace but battle, then let us fight each other personally."[7]

Historical literature tells us of more documents showing King George's dislike of war.[8] Indeed,

---

5] For utopias see most recently G. STRAUSS, "Siedlungs- und Architekturkonzeptionen der Utopisten," *Wissenschaftliche Zeitschrift der Humboldt-Universität zu Berlin, Gesellschafts- und sprachwissenschaftliche Reihe*, XI, 1962, 4, pp. 543—600.

6] This had already been pointed out by V. M. KORETSKI (see footnote No. 16 on p. 61), footnote No. 18.

7] *Archiv Český*, V, p. 307. — For related problems see K. G. CRAM, *Iudicium belli. Zum Charakter des Krieges im deutschen Mittelalter*, 1955; for a review of this book see the *Zeitschrift der Savigny-Stiftung für Rechtsgeschichte, Germ. Abt.* 74, 1957, pp. 324—327.

8] *Sitzungsberichte*, p. 30; R. URBÁNEK, *op. cit.*, 1962, pp. 160 *seq.*

it is a fact that most of the international treaties that he concluded dealt with the consolidation of peace. We are therefore not surprised to learn that the same rejection of war as a means of settling conflicts between states was characteristic of one of King George's most influential diplomats and military leaders, Albrecht Kostka of Postupice, who headed the Czech mission to France in 1464.

This, however, brings us to a set of especially complicated problems which have hitherto been so neglected in literature that in this respect we are truly at the very beginning of our scientific study. These problems concern a no less significant matter than determination of the social roots from which the ideas underlying the peace project of King George grew as well as the motives which caused these ideas to permeate the mind of the man who was known as one of the mightiest kings of Europe. Was it merely by chance that the project of the first universal organization of states for the safeguarding of peace was initiated by the ruler who is known as the "Hussite king" and whom, as we have already said, the Pope had condemned as a heretic? What were the circumstances which made it possible for the ideas contained in the project, whose timeliness we feel even today, to be introduced into European politics through official, diplomatic channels precisely from Bohemia which was still under the influence of the receding Hussite revolutionary movement? Is, perhaps, King George's peace project, which some modern authors consider phantastic and unrealistic, connected in some way with the Hussite traditions of responsibility for the future of the whole world, of concern for the welfare of all mankind, of struggle against imperial and papal universalism, and of eradication of what was then called the "secular rule of the clergy"?

The radical forms of the Hussite revolutionary movement were suppressed in the years 1434 to 1436, but the Hussite ideas were very much alive in one form or another in all the strata of Czech society, representing the growing Czech reformation which had sprung up half a century earlier in the form of a revolutionary movement. Although King George himself already represented the feudal lords in their determination to oppose in all respects the forces of social revolution represented by the radical Hussites, he nevertheless was at the same time — in the 1450's and 60's — the leading political representative of the Czech reformation in its then stage of development. At that time, radical trends were again beginning to gain ground among the broad masses of the people in Bohemia and Moravia, and especially in Prague.[9] The non-Catholic (Utraquist or Hussite) majority of the nation was angered by the steps taken by the Pope who once again tried to impose his will on the Czech State, regardless of the *Compactata* concluded with the representatives of Hussite Bohemia at the Church Council at Basle 30 years earlier. The Czechs again felt the danger that attempts would be made to eradicate even the little that remained as the outcome of the Hussite revolutionary movement. Specifically, they feared that communion in both kinds would be outlawed, that Church property and the political infuence of the clergy would be restituted, and that the Emperor and the Pope would again hinder the growth of the Czech Crown as an independent state.[10]

9] Regarding the excited mood prevailing in Bohemia and Moravia in the early 1460's see R. URBÁNEK, *op. cit.*, 1962, pp. 265—266, 471 and 564.

10] In this respect, the historical significance of King George's project stands out with particular clarity, when we realize that as late as at the end of that same, 15th century, the humanist scholar Konrad CELTES of Vienna, to mention one example, still dreamed of a reconstructed, world-wide Roman Empire centred on Germany. See J. ČELAKOVSKÝ in *Právník*, 1901, p. 695.

Inner connections with the Hussite revolutionary movement definitely exist and it is up to further historical research to define and elucidate them better than has been done thus far. However, we must not be prejudiced and one-sided and commit the error of seeing things in too simplified a manner. King George's project was probably influenced also by other spiritual trends whose social roots were chronologically and substantively very close to the Hussite movement, but which, nevertheless, had their own, specific nature which differed from the Hussite ideas. They too, must be pointed out, especially since they have been thus far completely ignored.

We should see that King George's project also has features which we cannot define otherwise that as those of the *Renaissance*, with all the pregnancy and vagueness of that term. The ideas on which the project is based no longer represent a blind belief in a set of fundamental dogmas served out to the faithful by the Church, but a belief in the omnipotence of human reason which is shedding the fetters of mediaeval scholasticism and drawing closer to nature and its order, but which — even in the eyes of the *Renaissance* thinkers — is still guided from some great distance by the unfathomable divine will. Courage to devise grandiose plans, confidence in a rational solution of even such extremely difficult social problems as are, still today, those of war, peace and international security, these are the main features which characterize King George's project as a product of the thinking of its time, of *Renaissance* thinking.[11]

And, finally, there is yet a third group of elements, which has also been somewhat ignored. What we have in mind is the interest in economic and financial questions represented by the provisions concerning uniform currency, universal law and controlled food prices, included in the project. We cannot but connect these elements with the interests of the new class arising in the late mediaeval society, the class of burghers and, among them, especially the merchants, financiers and enterpreneurs for whom the frontiers of the mediaeval states were too narrow and who showed truly cosmopolitan trends. There was nothing that could have met the interests of this then emerging class better than the project of a universal political organization safeguarding peace and security on a supranational basis.

Of course, we cannot isolate any of these three principal ideological components of King George's project. All three are combined and intertwined in the concept and composition of the project. The result is a remarkable synthesis, typical of 15th century Central Europe, dominated by Hussite elements which already represent the Reformation in its full development and expansion.

No doubt, the present outline of the problems yet to be studied could be augmented by a number of other important questions. However, we have limited ourselves to those which we consider to be the most vital, expressing at the same time the wish and the hope that the 500th anniversary of King George's project, which we are marking at a time when the struggle for lasting world peace has been taken up by the overwhelming majority of mankind, may spur the endeavour to elucidate this first attempt to establish a universal peace organization in the best possible, scholarly manner, so that it may become universally known not only in the countries where peace endeavours have a long-standing tradition, but also in countries where such a tradition is just being founded.

11] See František Šmahel, *Humanismus v době poděbradské* (Humanism in the Poděbrad Age), Rozpravy ČSAV, Řada společenských věd, 1963, No. 6.

TRACTATUS
PACIS
TOTI
CHRISTIANITATI
FIENDAE

EDIDIT

Jiří Kejř, JUDr., CSc.

TRACTATUS PACIS TOTI CHRISTIANITATI FIENDAE

I*n nomine Domini nostri Ihesu Cristi. Nos A B C notum facimus universis et singulis ad perpe-
tuam rei memoriam, quod, dum veterum historicorum scripta recensemus, reperimus cristianitatem
florentissimam quondam fuisse et hominibus opibusque beatam, cuius tanta longitudo latitudoque fuit,
ut in eius ventre centum decem et septem regna amplissima clauderentur, que eciam ex se tot populos
emisit, ut magnam gentilium partem una cum Dominico sepulcro longo tempore occuparit; nec gens
fuit tunc orbe toto, que cristianorum regimen lacessare auderet. At nunc quantum lacerata, confracta,
cassata atque omni nitore splendoreque pristino enudata sit, omnes agnoscimus. Tanta etenim mutacio
in ipsa cristianitate a paucis temporibus citra facta est, ut si quis regum, principum atque procerum
antiquorum iam ab inferis resurgeret et cristicolarum partes intraret, nullatenus suam propriam recog-
nosceret. Perfidus nempe Maumetus, cum pene universus orbis cristiane religionis sanctitate polleret,
principio gentem Arabum exiguam seduxit; verum ubi primis conatibus eius occurrere neglectum est,
continuo perditorum hominum tantam manum sibi acquisierat, ut latissimas Affrice pariter et Asie
regiones subiugavit et in dampnatissimam impulerit perfidiam. Spurcissimi denique Teucri, qui a
diebus paucissimis primo inclitum Grecorum imperium, deinde quamplures cristianitatis provincias et
regna in suam potestatem redigere, animas pene infinitas e cristianorum finibus asportarunt, omnia
in predam ducunt, plurima monasteria magnaque Dei templa demoliebantur et, ut ruerent, disposue-
runt; alia quoque infinita mala commiserunt et perpetraverunt.*

*O aurea provincia! O terrarum decus cristianitas, quomodo sic ex te nitor omnis abscessit, quo-
modo sic abiit color optimus? Ubi vigor ille tuorum hominum, ubi reverencia, quam tibi omnes gentes
impendebant, ubi maiestas regia, ubi gloria? Quid tibi tot victorie profuerunt, si tam cito in triumphum
duci debebas? Quid gentilium ducum restitisse potencie iuvat, si nunc vicinorum impetus ferre non
potes? Heu fortuna, heu vicissitudo! Quam cito imperia variantur, quam cito mutantur regna, quam
cito dilabuntur potestates! Que sit autem tante mutacionis ac ruine causa, non est intueri facile, quia
occulta sunt iudicia Dei. Non minus hodie quam olim fertiles sunt agri, non minus fecunda pecora,
assunt vinearum proventus, reddunt usuram effosse auri et argenti minere, sensati homines sunt, industri,
magnanimes, multarum rerum experti, littere tam vigent quam umquam. Quid enim est, quod cristiani-*

tatem adeo depressit, ut ex predictis centum decem et septem regnis dumtaxat in ventre cristianitatis sexdecim remanserint? Sunt fortasse nonnulla peccata, que Deus punire vult, quemadmodum in Veteri testamento nonumquam factum legimus? Ob quam rem nobis diligenter considerandum videtur, ut si quid erratum est, emendetur, et per opera pietatis divina maiestas mitigetur, quam propter iniquitatem aliquam constat iratam esse. Sed quia [cum] animadvertimus, quod cum hiis pie ac misericorditer Deus agat, quorum delicta in hoc mundo punit, quodque quod ipse homines pro filiis habet et quos diligit, corrigit et castigat per multasque adversitates ad opera virtutis inducit, ideo spem nostram iactantes in Dominum, cuius res agitur, scimus, quod sanctimonie nostre nil religiosius, integritati nil congruencius et laudi nil gloriosius efficere poterimus, quam dare operam, quod vera, pura et firma pax, unio et caritas inter cristianos fiat et fides Cristi adversus immanissimum Turcum defensetur. Ad hoc enim ad nos derivata sunt regna et principatus, ut solicitudine et diligencia nobis possibilibus pax decoretur, status rei publice sustentetur, bella adversus infideles feliciter peragantur et fines rei publice tueantur et propagentur; ad quas eciam res omnes populi, omnes naciones, omnesque reges et principes letis et promptis animis debent et tenentur intendere. Nam si cristianos nos dicimus, solicitudinem habere tenemur, ut cristiana religio tueatur; et si contra Cristum esse nolumus, pro fide sua certare et secum esse debemus. Spiritus enim Sanctus eos dampnat, qui secum in bello non sunt, qui ex adverso non ascendunt, qui se murum pro domo Israhel non ponunt. Nec aliquem patrie dulcedo, nec palacia amplissima, nec diviciarum multitudo a servicio Dei retrahere debent. Illi namque inserviendum erit, qui pro nobis mortem crucis subire non expavit, qui daturus est pro mercede unicuique fideli celi celorum patriam, ubi vera patria, ingencia habitacula, divicie incomparabiles et eterna vita consistit. Etenim quamvis hoc tempore lugubris sit fortuna Grecorum et dolenda nimis Constantinopolitana et aliarum provinciarum clades, nobis tamen, si glorie cupidi sumus, optanda fuit hec occasio, que nobis possit hoc decus reservare, ut defensores conservatoresque cristiani nominis appellaremur. Et ob id rei cupientes, ut talis modi bella, rapine, tumultus, incendia et cedes, que, ut prochdolor dolenter referimus, cristianitatem ipsam iam iam quasi undique circumdederunt, quibus agri vastantur, urbes diripiuntur, provincie lacerantur et innumeris regna ac principatus miseriis conteruntur, cessent et penitus extinguantur et ad statum debitum mutue caritatis et fraternitatis unione laudabili deducantur, nos de certa nostra sciencia, matura deliberacione prehabita, invocata ad hoc Spiritus Sancti gracia, prelatorum, principum, procerum, nobilium et iuris divini et humani doctorum nostrorum ad hoc accedente consilio et assensu, ad huiusmodi connexionis, pacis, fraternitatis et concordie inconcusse duraturam ob Dei reverenciam fideique conservacionem devenimus <in> unionem in modum, qui sequitur, pro nobis, heredibus et successoribus nostris futuris perpetuis temporibus duraturam.

[1]   Primo nempe in virtute fidei catolice et verbo regio et principis dicimus et pollicemur, quod ab hac hora et die inantea puram, veram et sinceram fraternitatem invicem exhibebimus et servabimus, nec propter quascunque dissensiones, querelas vel causas mutuo ad arma veniemus vel quoscunque nomine nostro venire permittemus, sed pocius unus

alium contra omnem hominem viventem et nos vel aliquem ex nobis de facto et absque legitimo edicto hostiliter invadere molientem iuxta continenciam et tenorem capitulorum subscriptorum iuvabimus.

[2] Secundo, quod nullus nostrum auxilium vel consilium dabit nec consenciet contra alterius personam neque in periculum seu necem persone ipsius per nos vel alium seu alios aliquatenus machinabimur aut de facto machinari volentibus consenciemus, sed conservacionem sanitatis, vite et honoris eiusdem pro posse procurabimus.

[3] Tercio, spondemus modo supradicto, quod si aliquis vel aliqui ex subditis cuiuscunque nostrum aliquas vastaciones, predas, rapinas, incendia aut alia quecunque maleficiorum genera in regnis, principatibus seu terris alterius nostrum commiserit vel commiserint, volumus, quod per hoc pax et unio premissa non sint violate nec infringantur, sed quod idem malefactores ad satisfaccionem, si amice fieri non poterit, iudicialiter compellantur ab eo, sub cuius dicione domicilium habuerint vel in cuius territorio delinquentes comperti fuerint, ita, quod dampna per ipsos facta de bonis eorum resarciantur et ipsi eciam alias pro qualitate delicti condigne puniantur. Qui malefactores, si iudicio parere contempserint, dominus eorum tam domicilii quam loci perpetrati delicti, quilibet eorum altero ad hoc eciam non expectato, ipsos tamquam maleficos persequi et impugnare tenebitur et debebit. Quod si aliquis nostrum, sub quo delinquens domicilium habuerit vel in cuius territorio delictum commissum et delinquens detentus fuerit, negligens et remissus in predictis extiterit, tunc, cum eum et delinquentem iure disponente par pena constringat, poterit iniuriam seu dampnum passus eundem ex nobis coram parlamento seu consistorio subscripto iudiciliater requirere et convenire.

[4] Quarto, volumus, quod si forte per aliquem seu aliquos extra hanc convencionem, caritatem et fraternitatem nostram existentes, a nobis non lacessitos nec provocatos, cuicunque ex nobis bellum inferretur seu inferri contingeret — quod minime verendum estimatur hac amicicia et caritate subsistente — tunc congregacio nostra subscripta nomine omnium in hoc federe existencium communibus nostris expensis, eciam a collega nostro oppresso non requisita, oratores suos sollempnes ad sedanda scandala pacemque componendam illico debet ad locum partibus accomodum transmittere et ibidem in presencia parcium dissidencium vel oratorum suorum pleno mandato suffultorum omni opera et diligencia dissidentes ad concordiam et pacem, si amice fieri poterit, revocare, vel ut ar-

bitros eligant vel coram iudice competenti vel parlamento vel consistorio modo sub-scripto de iure certent, inducere. Et si causa aut defectu bellum inferentis pax et unio altero eorum seu predictorum modorum fieri non poterit, nos ceteri omnes tunc unanimi ac concordi sentencia oppresso seu defendente(!) socio nostro ad sui defensionem ex decimis regnorum nostrorum et subditorum nostrorum proventibus, lucro seu emolu-mento, quos seu que ad usum domus et habitacionis sue pro tribus diebus proporcionabi-liter in anno exposuerint singulis annis, succurrere, quantum et quousque ab eadem con-gregacione nostra vel maiori parte ipsius iudicatum et decretum fuerit fore condecens et opportunum ad pacem oppressi socii consequendam.

[5] Utque diffidaciones et bella, que per suam consideracionem inter suscipientes alterutros operantur dolores, amplius arceantur et inter reliquos Cristi fideles, de hoc federe non existentes, eciam pax vigeat, volumus et ordinamus, quod si forsan contingeret alios principes et magnates cristicolas fraternitati nostre non incorporatos inter se dissensio-nibus aut bello certare, ex tunc congregacio nostra subscripta nostris nominibus per oratores deputandos communibus nostris expensis concordiam amice vel in iure, ut pre-fertur, inter differentes pro posse efficiat. Quam si ambe partes vel una earum eodem modo acceptare et a bellis et a guerris desistere noluerint vel noluerit, ex tunc bellum inferens vel a bello desistere nolens inducatur modis et formis in capitulo supra proximo insertis.

[6] Item volumus, quod illi, qui pacem nostram presentem quovismodo violare temptaverint, in nullius nostrum regno, principatibus, dominiis, territoriis et districtibus, castris, civi-tatibus, oppidis seu fortaliciis receptari, conduci, protegi, tueri vel aliquem favorem quovis quesito colore habere debebunt seu poterunt; quinimmo non obstante quocunque salvo conductu arrestabuntur, capientur et punientur ut violatores pacis generalis, prout quali-tas delicti seu excessus cuiuslibet eorum meruerit.

[7] Volumus preterea et presentibus iniungimus omnibus et singulis officialibus et subditis nostris, ut nullum umquam hominem in eorum proteccionem et tuicionem communiter vel divisim recipiant vel illi salvum conductum generalem vel specialem quovismodo concedant vel prestent, nisi per prius particulariter et nominatim excipiant, quod salvus conductus sive proteccio ista non debeant eum, cui dantur, contra presentis nostre pacis edicta tueri et defendere, sed eo non obstante, si de violacione pacis infamatus, suspectus

vel accusatus fuerit, poterit supra hoc contra eum, ut prefertur, et eciam iusticia mediante procedi.

[8] Qui autem violatorem pacis presentis scienter sociaverit aut ei quovis quesito colore consilium, auxilium vel favorem prestiterit vel eum receptaverit aut ipsum defendere seu protegere vel ei salvum conductum contra presentem nostram unionem dare presumpserit, par pena ipsum et reum expectet.

[9] Verum cum pacis cultus a iusticia et iusticia ab illo esse non possit et per iusticiam pax gignitur et conservatur, nec sine illa nos et subditi nostri in pace subsistere poterimus, ob id rei paci iusticiam annectimus. Sed cum lex, que de iudiciorum ordine scripta est, multas mutaciones subsequentibus temporibus susceperat, ad hoc pervenit, ut paulatim omnino caderet, unde usus hoc precipiens in aliam transtulit figuram, propter que nos omnino confusum iudiciorum ordinem considerantes estimamus opportere iuxta novorum temporum et diversarum provinciarum, regnorum et principatuum nostrorum consuetudines, usus et qualitates de nature gremio nova iura producere et novis abusibus nova remedia reperire, per que virtuosi ditentur premiis et viciosi continuis penarum maleis conterantur. Et ut secundum ordinem singula tractemus, previdimus primitus ordinare quoddam generale consistorium, quod omnium nostrorum et tocius congregacionis nostre nomine in loco, ubi congregacio ipsa pro tempore fuerit, observetur, a quo veluti a fonte iusticie rivuli undique deriventur. Quod quidem iudicium ordinabitur in numero et qualitate personarum et statutorum, prout subscripta nostra congregacio vel maior pars eiusdem concluserit et decreverit.

[10] Et ut in eodem iudicio finis litibus imponatur, ne immortales sint, volumus, quod iudex ipse et assessores eiusdem conquerentibus, prout causarum qualitates postulaverint, iudicium et iusticiam faciant simpliciter et de plano sine figura et strepitu iudicii, subterfugiis et frustratoriis dilacionibus omnino cessantibus.

[11] Placet preterea, quod, si quas querelas et differencias de novo inter nos reges et principes aliosque in federe isto existentes suboriri contingat, quod alteri alter coram dicto iudicio

nostro in iure respondere et secum experiri debeat et teneatur, servatis in hoc statutis, decretis et ordinacionibus per oratores et procuratores nostros vel maiorem partem eorundem in congregacione ipsa, ut prefertur, faciendis et statuendis.

[12] Item volumus eciam, quod congregacio nostra debeat habere omnimodam et liberam facultatem quoscunque reges, principes et magnates cristianos, qui de presenti huic unioni incorporati non fuerint, ad presentem nostram pacem, unionem, caritatem et fraternitatem accipiendi et sese nomine nostro, quemadmodum nos ipsi fecimus, obligandi et reciproca vicissitudine obligaciones accipiendi litteris opportunis, ultro citroque datis et acceptis, hoc tamen adiecto, quod mox acceptacione tali facta congregacio ipsa nobis omnibus significet, ut acceptos ad nos fraternali affeccione, ut decet, perpetrare valeamus et possimus.

[13] Ceterum cum hec unio, intelligencia et caritas potissime facta sit et constituatur ad gloriam et honorem divine maiestatis, sancte Romane ecclesie ac catolice fidei et ut potissime hiis Cristi fidelibus celerrime succurratur, qui a Teucrorum principe, cristiani nominis hoste sevissimo, deprimuntur, idcirco nos prefati reges et principes promittimus ac devovimus Domino nostro Ihesu Cristo, eius gloriosissime matri Virgini Marie, sancteque Romane ecclesie cristianam religionem ac universos fideles oppressos defensare ac protegere a spurcissimo Teucrorum principe communibus inter nos viribus et presidiis proporcionabiliter taxandis et declarandis, pro quibus conficiendis et exequendis omnes decimas, que ecclesiis ecclesiasticisque et religiosis personis in regnis, principatibus et dominiis nostris dantur et solvuntur, una cum dictis nostris et subditorum nostrorum proventibus, lucris et emolumentis pro tribus diebus, ut prefertur, singulis annis exponendis, quoadusque opus fuerit, soluturos et daturos atque ab hostis insecucione non destituros, si a congregacione nostra expediens iudicabitur, quoadusque a cristianorum finibus fuerit effugatus aut communi sentencia pax conficienda censeatur, que nulla racione confici debet, nisi finitimorum securitati cristianorum ante cautum fore iudicabitur.

[14] Preterea cum omnia solerti studio ac diligencia ante cavenda sint, ne incautos demum adversa fortuna contendat, ideo placet nobis, quod communi sentencia tocius congregacionis nostre vel maioris partis eiusdem discernatur, quibus temporibus hostem aggredi expediat quibusve terrestribus ac maritimis copiis bellum gerere opus sit quibusve belli ducibus, quibus machinis bellicisve apparatibus uti necesse sit, quo in loco omnes exerci-

tus terrestres convenire debeant ulterius contra Turcos profecturi. Item quomodo victualia haberi possint in competenti precio et hospicia in civitatibus, villis et allis locis opportunis. Item quomodo provideatur de communi moneta, per quam in exercitu venientes in eundo, stando et redeundo non graventur. Item si quid ex hostium manibus aut potestate adimi ulla racione contingeret, communi sentencia, cui conferendum fuerit, decernatur, prout utilius cristiane religioni et ad maiorem fidelium tutelam in posterum convenire cognitum et iudicatum fuerit, ne hostis denuo negligencia aut impotencia possidencium excitatus deteriora prioribus detrimenta fidelibus inferat.

[15]   Volumus preterea, quod conclusis istis mox quilibet nostrum ad pecuniarum exacciones, ut prefertur, in regno, principatu et dominio suo procedat iuxta formam et ordinem a congregacione ipsa vel maiori eius parte dandam in finem, ut divinum hoc opus illico exequatur et Cristi fidelibus succurratur.

[16]   Item, ut supra et infra scripta omnia et singula debite execucioni demandentur, promittimus et pollicemur modo predicto, quod quilibet nostrum oratores suos notabiles et magne auctoritatis viros amplissimo mandato et sigillo suo suffultos dominica Reminiscere de anno a nativitate Domini millesimo quadringentesimo sexagesimo quarto proxime futura in civitate Basiliensi in Theotonia habeat, qui omnes ibidem ad quinquennium immediate sequens continuum resideant et nostris et aliorum incorporatorum seu incorporandorum nominibus corpus, universitatem seu collegium verum faciant, constituant et representent. Quo quidem quinquennio congregacionis Basiliensis effluxo eadem congregacio per aliud immediatum sequens quinquennium in civitate N in Francia et per tercium quinquennium in civitate N in Italia habeatur et observetur sub eisdem modis et condicionibus, quibus supra de Basilia cautum et dispositum dinoscitur, ut deinceps semper de quinquennio ad quinquennium circuitum faciendo tamdiu et quousque ipsa congregacio vel maior pars eiusdem aliud duxerit ordinandum et disponendum. Unum quoque proprium et speciale consilium ipsa congregacio habeat, cuius presidens, pater et caput N et nos ceteri cristianitatis reges et principes membra simus. Habeat eciam dictum collegium in nos omnes et nostros subditos eosque, qui eandem prorogaverint, iurisdiccionem voluntariam et contenciosam una cum mero et mixto imperio, prout eadem congregacio vel maior pars eiusdem hoc decreverit et statuerit ordinandum. Habeat denique propria arma, sigillum et archam communem atque archivum publicum, sindicum, fiscalem, officiales et quecunque alia iura ad licitum et iustum collegium quomodolibet pertinencia et spectancia.

[17]   Et ut unicuique provincie iura sua illesa conserventur, placeat nobis, quod tales in con-
         gregacione pocioribus officiis in qualibet nacione, in qua congregacio ipsa pro tempore
         fuerit, preficiantur, qui de eadem nacione ortum et originem traxerint moresque et habitu-
         dines ipsius agnoscant et intelligant.

[18]   Porro, ut expense et sumptus necessarie [et] utiles pro pace servanda, iusticia ministranda,
         oratoribus et nunciis hicinde transmittendis, designandis et aliis opportunitatibus con-
         gregacioni nostre non deficiant, promittimus et spondemus, quod quilibet nostrum deci-
         mam partem omnium pecuniarum per eum seu suo nomine de decimis et emolumento
         seu lucro trium dierum, ut prefertur, sublevandarum in tempore per congregacionem
         ipsam vel maiorem partem eius determinando ad archivum publicum collectoribus et
         consilio dicte congregacionis absque ulteriori mora deleget et transmittat. Quod si non
         fecerit, poterit et debebit ipsum sindicus seu procurator fiscalis eiusdem congregacionis
         mox coram parlamento seu iudicio ipsius in ius vocare, pecuniam cum dampnis et interesse
         iudicialiter requirere et eciam nos alios sub debito per nos prestito fidei monere et hortari,
         ut dictam pecuniam, dampna et interesse manu militari ab eo et subditis suis requiramus
         et extorqueamus in usus communes congregacionis, ut prefertur, convertendas.

[19]   Rursum dicimus et volumus, quod nos rex Francie una cum ceteris regibus et principibus
         Gallie unam, nos vero reges et principes Germanie aliam et nos dux Veneciarum una cum
         principibus, communitatibus Italie terciam vocem in ipsa congregacione habeamus et
         faciamus. Ac si rex Castelle vel alii nacionis Hispanie reges et principes in hac nostra
         unione, amicicia et fraternitate concurrerint, ipsi consimiliter unam vocem in congrega-
         cione, corpore et collegio ipso habebunt. Si autem inter oratores regum et principum
         unius et eiusdem nacionis contraria vota super re aliqua data et conclusa fuerint, placet,
         ut quod a maiori parte dictum et conclusum sit, perinde firmitate subsistat, ac si ab ipsa
         nacione unanimi assensu iudicatum et decretum extitisset. Quod si equales persone nume-
         ro in voto fuerint, prevaleant illi oratores, qui comparacione facta ad alios per represen-
         tacionem dominorum suorum maiorum meriti et dignitatis fuerint. Et si in meritis et
         dignitatibus equales sint, opcio erit aliarum nacionum in hoc federe existencium, quam
         partem acceptarint.

[20]   Et ut dubietas omnino tollatur, placet, ut si aliquis regum vel principum nostrorum plures
         oratores ad dictam congregacionem transmiserit, quod hi omnes dumtaxat habeant unicam,
         videlicet ipsius mittentis in nacione sua dicte congregacionis vocem.

[21] Item, cum Scriptura testatur, ei, qui fidem Cristi iuverit, auxerit, defenderit, diffinitum esse locum in celo, in quo beati evo sempiterno fruuntur, proinde sperandum est, quod omnes ceteri cristiani ad rem tam sanctam, tam piam, tam necessariam volentibus animis manus apponent. Nam qui prestare auxilia hoc tempore contra Turcos negaverit, infidelitatis proculdubio et inimicorum crucis Cristi fautorem se declarabit. Et ob id rei placet, quod nos omnes unanimiter per sollempnes oratores nostros apud summum pontificem omni opera et diligencia nobis possibilibus sub modis et formis per congregacionem predictam dandis efficiamus, ut Sanctitas sua attendat, quod exaccio supradicta decimarum ad tuendam cristianorum pacem, Cristi fidelium defensionem et inimicorum crucis Cristi impugnacionem exposcatur, et tamquam pater et pastor fidelium de benignitatis sue clemencia concedat et demandet per suas publicas et autenticas bullas sub formidabilibus penis executoribus sibi nominandis superinde in plenissima forma datis et deputatis, quod decime prefate iuxta modum et condiciones sibi nostris nominibus offerendas dentur, tradantur et exolvantur utque bella et dissensiones inter principes ecclesiasticos et in hoc federe non existentes et — potissime illa, que <ad> bella in Turcos conficienda et pace predicta conservanda quoquomodo impedimento esse possent — e medio tollat vel legatum aliquem virum utique bone vite, probum et expertum, cum plenaria ad hoc facultate ad unamquamque provinciam transmittat, qui ritum, idioma et habitudines eiusdem intelligat et agnoscat operamque et diligenciam condignas adhibeat, ut partes differentes amice componantur; quod si facere noluerit, differencias inter eos pendentes in vim commissionis sibi facte in iure diffiniat et decidat. Convocet denique Sanctitas sua alios principes et communitates Italie et eosdem sub divinis censuris et formidabilibus penis moneat et requirat, ut ipsi tamquam Turco pre ceteris nacionibus magis vicini ad instruendam classem maritimam una cum aliis cristicolis assurgant, illis proporcionabilia presidia ad honorem et gloriam Dei fideliumque defensionem conferant ac contribuant, ut hoc opus defendende fidei speratum finem eo laudabilius accipiat.

[22] Preterea, ut pax et ordinacio ista inviolabiliter observetur, decrevimus ac pollicemur, ut quocunque ex nobis ad celestem patriam evocato heredum sive successorum suorum nulli in regno, principatu seu dominio suo succedere liceat neque ad hoc admitti debeat, nisi prius sese supra et infra scripta omnia et singula inviolabili fide servaturum spondeat litteris suis patentibus cum sigillo appenso congregacioni nostre tamquam communibus munimentis ad usum cuiuslibet nostrum datis.

[23] Et si aliqua alia ultra premissa dicta nostra congregacio vel maior pars eiusdem ordinaverit, decreverit et concluserit, que pro conservacione pacis et iusticie fideliumque cristi-

colarum defensione facere et conducere quomodolibet videbuntur, illa omnia et singula attendemus et efficaciter observabimus atque id agemus, que vere et sincere fraternitatis vinculum exigit et requirit et que in presentibus litteris nostris per diffiniciones et continencias earundem in suis punctis, clausulis, articulis, sentenciis quoque et capitulis universis comprehenduntur.

In cuius rei testimonium et robur quilibet rex et principum nostrorum sigillum maiestatis sue presentibus duxit appendendum. Datum et actum etc.

EDITORIAL NOTE

This edition of the peace proposals of King George of Bohemia has been prepared on the basis of five manuscripts:

[1]   WARSAW, Archiwum główne akt dawnych, *Metryka koronna*, Vol. XI, pp. 578—587. — The text of the document was probably transcribed immediately upon its delivery to the Polish court and must be taken as the basic source of research not only because it was copied from the original for the purposes of the Polish Royal Chancellery and is chronologically closest to the time of origin of King George's project, but also because its wording is reliable and exact. The scribe who copied the text did make some minor mistakes either by omitting a word or by erroneous transcription, it is true, but none of them is of a fundamental nature and can be easily detected and corrected with the help of the other manuscripts. — The text of the document is introduced with these headings: *Secuntur articuli in eodem facto tractatus pacis toti cristianitati fiende, regi Polonie missi.* — *Serenissimo ac potentissimo regi Polonie per me Anthonium Marini indignum consiliarium et oratorem cristianissimi regis Francorum necnon sereni regis Bohemie.*

[2]   KLAGENFURT, Episcopal Library, MS XXX c 29, fol. 183r — 190r. — The manuscript contains the complete text which, in its contents and division, is identical to manuscript No. 1, but has more errors in transcription; however, these do not affect the continuity and sense of the document. A date is attached at the end: *Anno domini M CCCC° LXIIII°.* *Et sic est finis huius.*

[3]   PARIS, Bibliothèque Nationale, MS N.A. fr. 7973, fol. 9r—18r. — The text is complete and reliable and corresponds in its inner division to manuscript No. 1. It was transcribed from a good copy with only minor errors.

[4]   GDAŃSK, Biblioteka Polskiej Akademii Nauk, MS 2031, fol. 361r—367v. — This manuscript is not complete owing to its first page being missing. The text therefore begins with the words *delicta in hoc mundo punit* (here on p. 70). The sequence of paragraphs is also different: paragraph 4 ends with the words *suorum pleno mandato* (here on p. 71), and is followed by paragraphs 8—11. Then the rest of paragraph 4 follows as a separate paragraph, beginning with the words *suffultorum omni opera*, and paragraphs 5—7. The text then continues with paragraph 12 without interruption to the

end. — The text itself shows some errors in transcription, most probably due to the copy from which it was transcribed, but in this manuscript, too, the form and sense of the original have been preserved rather well and can be used for checking and reconstruction of the correct version of the original.

[5]   PARIS, Bibliothèque Nationale, MS Fr. 6971, fol. 336v — 340r. — A late copy dating from the 17th century. The actual text is preceded by the designation of the collection *Dupuy 760* and the date *1464*. A younger hand inscribed above it the date *18. Juillet 1464*. Also included is the title of the whole document, *Traité d'alliance et confédération entre le Roy Louys XI, George Roy de Bohême et la Seigneurie de Venise pour résister au Turc.* — It should be noted that in the opening of the document, the sentence *Nos A B C* is replaced by *Nos G R B*, which is probably due to misunderstanding on the part of the 17th century scribe or to insufficient legibility of the copy from which the transcript was made. It is from this manuscript that the name of King George was mistakenly presented as the author of the project *Nos Georgius Rex Bohemiae* in the oldest edition of Lenglet and the editions derived from it, although actually it was only an error of the late scribe who obviously deviated from the original and which opposed the nature of the project as a draft of the planned multilateral treaty.

TREATY ON THE ESTABLISHMENT OF PEACE THROUGHOUT CHRISTENDOM

In the name of our Lord Jesus Christ. We A B C. Let this be known to one and all for eternity: We learn from the writings of ancient historians that Christianity once flourished and was blessed with men and goods, spreading so far and wide that it held in its womb one hundred and seventeen rich kingdoms, that it also brought forth so many people that for a long time it held a large part of pagandom including the Holy Sepulchre; in those days there was no nation in the world which would have dared to challenge Christian rule. But we all know how lacerated it is today, how broken, impoverished and deprived of all its former brilliance and splendour it is. For not long ago Christendom passed through such a change that if any of the ancient kings, princes or notables were to rise from the dead and visit the Christian countries, he would not recognise his very own land. When almost the whole world was strong with the holiness of the Christian religion, the astute Mohammed first led astray the exiguous Arab nation. However, when his first attempts were not opposed, he gradually acquired so many of the lost people that he subjugated very large regions of Africa and Asia and incited them to commit a most detestable treachery. And then the utterly despicable Turks, who had most recently subjugated first the famous Greek Empire and then very many Christian lands and kingdoms, abducted an almost innumerable multitude of souls from the Christian parts, took away everything as bounty, destroyed and defiled many convents and large churches, and perpetrated very many other evils.

Oh, golden land! Oh, Christianity, Thou jewel of all lands, how could all Thy glory disappear in such a way, how couldst Thou lose all Thy most magnificent brilliance? Where is the vigour of all Thy people, where is the reverence shown to Thee by all nations, where is Thy royal glory, Thy fame? What good were Thy many victories when so soon Thou werest to be led in a triumphal march? What good does it serve that Thou hast resisted the power of pagan leaders when now Thou art unable to resist the attacks of Thy neighbours? Woe to fate! Woe to vicissitude! How quickly empires change, how quickly kingdoms succeed each other, how quickly governments deteriorate! It is indeed not easy to understand the cause of such change and ruin because the Lord's designs are hidden. The fields are still as ripe as they used to be, just as prolific are the herds, the vineyards are fruitful, profits flow in from the goldfields and silver mines, men are sensible, industrious, brave and expert in many things, *letters flourish as never before. What is it, then, that has so depraved Christianity that only sixteen of the said one hundred and seventeen kingdoms are left in the womb of Christendom? It must be the many sins that God wants to punish as so often before, to which the Old Testament bears witness. Therefore it seems to us that due consideration should be paid to amending what may be erroneous and to mollifying His Divine Majesty with pious acts, as it apparently must be ired by some ill deed. However, since we know that God deals justly and mercifully with those whose wrongs He punishes in this world and that He considers men his sons and those whom He loves He corrects, castigates and leads to virtue through many adversities, we hold, turning our hopes to our Lord whose cause is at stake, that we can do nothing more pious in our integrity, nothing more compatible with our honesty and nothing more glorious for our praise than to strive diligently for the establishment among Christians of true, pure and lasting peace, unity and love, and to defend the faith of Christ against the most vicious Turk. For we have been entrusted with the rule of kingdoms and principalities in order to glorify peace with all possible care and diligence, to uphold the position of Christendom, to bring the wars against the infidel to a successful end, and to guard and extend the frontiers of Christendom; these aims should and must be striven for by all men, all nations and all kings and princes with a joyous and ready mind. For if we call ourselves Christians, we must see to it that the Christian religion is protected; if we do not want to be against Christ, we must fight for His faith and stand with Him. For the Holy Spirit damns those who do not fight on His side, who do not oppose the enemy, who do not stand up like a wall to protect the House of Israel. And no man must be detracted from service to God by the sweetness of his land or magnificent palaces or a multitude of wealth. For we must serve Him, who was not afraid to die for us on the cross, who will reward every believer with the heavenly realm which is our true home, offering an endless abode, incomparable riches and eternal life. And thus, although the fate of the Greeks at this time is sorrowful and although we must loudly mourn the disaster of Constantinople and other lands, we can but rejoice, if we crave for glory, in this opportunity which will allow us to call ourselves defenders and preservers of the Christian name. Therefore, desiring that such wars, plunder, tumult, fires and murders which, alas, have engulfed Christendom almost on all sides, which devastate fields, destroy towns, lacerate lands and ruin through endless miseries kingdoms and principalities, should end and be completely eradicated and that such kingdoms and principalities may be brought through praiseworthy unity into a state of mutual charity and fraternity, we have decided on the basis of reliable knowledge, after thorough preliminary consideration, having prayed to the Holy Spirit for guidance and after consulting and gaining the consent of our prelates, princes, notables, noblemen and doctors of divine and human law, to create such a bond of alliance and degree of fraternity and concord as would endure and last forever for us, our heirs and future successors in the forms indicated below:*

[1]   First of all, we hereby declare and pledge on the honour of the Catholic faith and upon our royal and princely word that from this hour and day on we shall extend to one another and maintain pure, true and sincere fraternity, that we shall not resort to arms

or allow any man to resort to them in our name due to any dissension, quarrel or complaint, but rather that we shall support one another, in accordance with the letter and spirit of the further described provisions, against any living man who might try to attack us or any one of us by a hostile act and without a legitimate edict.

[2] Secondly, that none of us shall grant assistance or advice, or associate against the person of any other of us, and that we neither ourselves nor through another or others shall in any manner whatsoever conspire to endanger or cause the death of any other of us, nor shall we associate with those who would plot unlawful machinations, but that we shall care as much as possible for the maintenance of the health, life and honour of the others.

[3] Thirdly, we pledge in the aforesaid manner that if one or some of the subjects of any one of us commit some devastation, plunder, robbery, arson or other crimes in the kingdoms, principalities or provinces of any other of us, our will is that the said peace and unity will thereby not be abolished or broken, but that such malefactors will be forced by him within whose area of jurisdiction they reside or on whose territory they are discovered as delinquents to give satisfaction voluntarily or in court, so that the damage caused by them will be compensated from their property, they themselves to be duly punished in accordance with the nature of their crime; those criminals held in contempt of court shall be pursued and prosecuted by their lords, both according to their domicile and the place of the committed crime, without such lords waiting for the other to take action. If any of us, in whose territory the delinquent is domiciled or on whose territory the crime is committed and the delinquent detained, neglects and fails to proceed as provided above, the person who has suffered injustice or damage may prosecute and sue such one of us in the below described parliament or consistory, because under the law he and the delinquent should suffer the same penalty.

[4] Fourthly, we provide that if some person or persons standing outside this covenant and our charity and fraternity, without having been injured by us or without having been provoked, should begin war against any of us, or intend to begin it (which we need not fear, if this amity and charity persist), our below described assembly shall dispatch in the name of all the parties to the present covenant and at our joint expense, even if the attacked companion does not so request, its solemn envoys to settle the dispute and restore peace to a place suitable to the parties, and there, in the presence of the parties in dispute or

their envoys invested with full powers, they shall diligently strive to bring the parties in dispute to concord and peace through friendship, if possible, or persuade them to appoint arbitrators or seek justice before a competent judge or parliament or consistory in the below described manner. And if owing to the person who started the war, or through his fault, peace and unity cannot be obtained by negotiation, all of us shall help our attacked or self-defending companion by unanimous and concordant decision to defend himself from the tithes of our kingdoms and from the incomes, profits, and yields of our subjects which they spend on their homes and households on the average in three days of every year, in such a sum and for such a time as this our assembly or its majority may decide and determine as being proportionate and suitable for our attacked companion to obtain peace.

[5]   In order to facilitate the suppression of dissidence and wars, the very thought of which pains those who have to experience them, and in order to strengthen peace also among others faithful to Christ who are not parties to the present covenant, we hereby provide and order that if discord or war should occur between other Christian princes and magnates who are not included in our fraternity, our below described assembly shall dispatch in our name and at our mutual expense envoys whose task will be to restore concord between the parties in dispute, if possible by friendly means, or by way of law, as stated above; if both parties or one of them do not wish to be reconciled and to desist from fighting and wars, the person who started the war or who does not wish to desist from it shall be brought to order in the manner and forms described in the preceding article.

[6]   We provide further that those who dare in any manner whatsoever disturb our present peace must not and cannot be received, employed, protected, supported or granted any favour under any pretense whatsoever in any of our kingdoms, principalities, estates, territories and districts, castles, towns, villages or forts; instead, irrespective of any letter of safe conduct they may possess, they shall be arrested, captured and punished as violators of general peace in accordance with the nature of their crime or excess, as each of them merits.

[7]   Furthermore, we provide and hereby order our officials and subjects, all and each separately, never to take any man under their protection and tuition — jointly or individually — and in no manner whatsoever to grant him a general or special letter of safe conduct

without reserving in advance, particularly and expressly, that such letter of safe conduct or protection will not protect and guard the person to whom it is issued against the measures of our present peace, so that if he is accused and suspected of or indicted for violating the peace, action may be taken against him in the above stated manner without any hindrance, including the process of justice.

[8] Whosoever knowingly associates with a violator of the present peace and under any pretense whatsoever grants him counsel, assistance or favour, or receives him, or dares to protect or defend him or issue him a letter of safe conduct contrary to our present union, shall himself be punished by the same penalty as the culprit.

[9] As the cult of peace is unthinkable without justice, and justice without such endeavours, because peace is born of justice and is upheld by it, and because we and our subjects cannot subsist in peace without justice, we link justice with the cause of peace; however, because the law written on judicial matters has undergone many changes in the passing of time, having reached the stage where it has gradually lost all its significance and has been given a completely different interpretation in practice, we consider judicial procedure to be utterly confused and hold that in accordance with the customs, usages and conditions of the new times and of our various provinces, kingdoms and principalities, new laws drawn from the heart of the nature must be introduced and that new evils must be opposed by new remedies under which the virtuous will be rewarded and the vicious constantly crushed under the hammer of penalties. And in order to settle individual matters in proper order, we have decided, first of all, to establish a single general consistory which will sit in the name of all of us and our whole assembly at the place where the assembly is sitting at that time, and from it, as from a spring, rivulets of justice will flow to all sides. This court shall be established in accordance with what our below described assembly or its majority may conclude and decide with respect to the number of its members, their qualification, and the rules of its procedure.

[10] And in order that disputes be brought to an end in this court and not be protracted indefinitely, we hereby will that in accordance with the nature of the dispute, the judge himself and the assessors conduct the proceedings for the parties in dispute and find justice simply and clearly, without formalities and judicial clamour, by disposing of all subterfuges and frustrating delays.

[11]   We resolve further that if disputes and quarrels newly occur between us, the kings and princes and the other parties to our covenant, we shall be duty bound and obliged to one another to answer before our court in conformity with the law, and to conduct the dispute there, and in doing so to observe the statutes, decrees and orders issued and decreed by our spokesmen and representatives in the assembly, or their majority, as stated above.

[12]   We will also that our assembly should have full and unrestricted freedom to admit to our present peace, union, charity and fraternity any Christian kings, princes and magnates, who at present are not incorporated in this union, through proper letters mutually given and accepted, and in our name, as if we ourselves had done so, to undertake and accept obligations of mutual friendship with the proviso that as soon as such acceptance is carried out, the assembly itself shall duly notify all of us, so that we may deal with the newly admitted party with due and proper fraternal affection.

[13]   As this union, understanding and charity have been constituted and established mainly for the glory and honour of the Divine Majesty, the Holy Roman Church and the Catholic faith, and also in order to help as quickly as possible those faithful to Christ who are being oppressed by the prince of the Turks, the severest enemy of the Christian name, we, the above kings and princes, pledge and swear to our Lord Jesus Christ, to His most glorious Mother, the Virgin Mary, and to the Holy Roman Church that we shall defend and protect the Christian religion and all the oppressed faithful against the vilest prince of the Turks with our joint forces and means which will be proportionately determined and declared, and which we shall secure by returning and giving, if necessary, all the tithes which are paid to the churches as well as to the ecclesiastic and religious persons in our kingdoms, principalities and dominions, together with the said incomes, profits and yields coming to us and our subjects, which are, as stated above, spent on three days of each year, and we shall not cease to pursue the enemy, if our assembly deems it expedient, until he is driven out of Christian territory or until it is jointly resolved to conclude peace, which may be done only if the security of neighbouring Christians is deemed ensured.

[14]   Furthermore, as it is necessary to avoid in advance skilfully and diligently all that might bring ill fortune to the incautious, we hereby resolve that our whole assembly or its majority shall determine when it is suitable to attack the enemy or what land and naval

forces should be used to conduct the war, or under which generals this should be done, what machines or instruments of war should be used, and at what place all the land forces should assemble that will march against the Turks. Also, in what manner it would be possible to obtain at decent prices victuals and billets in towns, villages and other suitable places. Also, in what manner a common coin should be provided so that the troops would not find themselves in difficulties on the march, when billeting and on their return. Also, if it is judged and recognised that in the future the Christian religion and the greater safety of the faithful would benefit therefrom, a joint decision shall determine who should be given what, if something should be successfully acquired from the enemy's possession and power, so that the enemy, once again encouraged by the negligence or inability of the possessors, does not cause the faithful new detriment, even worse than that preceding it.

[15] We will further that as soon as it is so resolved, every one of us should immediately begin the above described collection of money in his kingdom, principality and dominion in a manner and form to be determined by the assembly or its majority for the instant execution of this divine work and for helping the faithful in Christ.

[16] Moreover, in order to ensure due execution of all that is written above and below, in total, and in its individual parts, we undertake and pledge in the above described manner that every one of us shall have his envoys, who shall be men of importance and high repute, invested with the fullest of powers and our seal, come not later than on the next Sunday *Reminiscere* in the year of our Lord one thousand four hundred and sixty-four to the city of Basle in Germany; where they shall be in constant residence for the immediately following quinquennium and in our name and the name of the other members or those desirous of being admitted into the union shall form, constitute and represent a body, corporation or regular college. And after the end of such a quinquennial assembly in Basle, the same assembly shall be held and sit for the next, immediately following quinquennium in the city of N in France, and for the third quinquennium in the city of N in Italy in the same manner and under the same conditions as resolved and decreed above; then, always after five years, it shall change its seat until such time as the assembly itself or its majority may resolve and decide otherwise. The assembly shall have its own and special council whose president shall be N as its father and head, and we, the other Christian kings and princes, shall be its members. The said college shall also have voluntary and contentious jurisdiction with pure and mixed authority over all of us and our subjects as well as those who voluntarily submit thereto, as the present assembly or its

majority may decide and decree. Finally, it shall have its own coat-of-arms, seal and common treasury as well as public archives, a syndic, a fiscal, clerks, and all the other rights allowed and appertaining to a proper corporation.

[17]   And in order that every province may preserve intact its rights, we resolve that in every nation where the assembly is residing at a particular time, men born of such nation who know and understand its mores and customs, shall be appointed to head the higher offices of the assembly.

[18]   Finally, so that our assembly does not lack funds to meet the expenses and costs necessary and useful for the maintenance of peace, the administration of justice, the designation and dispatch of envoys and messengers to all parties as well as for other needs, we pledge and undertake that every one of us shall without further delay send and transfer to the public archives through the hands of the collectors and the council of the said assembly a tenth part of all the monies which are to be collected by him or in his name from the tithes and three-day yields or profits, as stated above, at a time decided on by the assembly or its majority. And if he fails to do so, the syndic or the fiscal procurator of the assembly may and must immediately sue him in its parliament or court and judicially enforce the payment of the money, including damages and interest, and warn and urge the others of us, who are bound by the pledge given on our faith, to enforce the payment of such money, damages and interest from him and his subjects by military force so that they may be expended on the common needs of the assembly, as stated above.

[19]   We further declare and will that in this assembly we, the King of France together with the other kings and princes of Gaul, shall have and constitute one vote, we, the kings and princes of Germany, the second vote, and we, the Doge of Venice together with the princes and cities of Italy, the third vote. And if this our union, amity and fraternity is joined by the King of Castille or the other kings and princes of the Hispanic nation, they shall similarly have one vote in the assembly, corporation and college. However, if among the envoys sent by the kings and princes of one and the same nation an opposing opinion should arise on a certain matter, it is hereby decreed that what the majority recognises and resolves shall be valid as if their very nation had so decided and ordered by unanimous approval. Should there be equal votes, those envoys shall prevail who, compared with the others, enjoy greater prominence due to the greater merits and dignity

of the lords whom they represent. And if they should be equal in merits and dignity, it shall be left to the other nations associated under this covenant to decide which side they will favour.

[20] In order to eliminate any doubt, it is hereby resolved that if any of our kings dispatches several envoys to the said assembly, all of them shall have only one vote, that is the vote of their sender in the national curia of the said assembly.

[21] Moreover, as the Holy Scripture testifies to the fact that whoever helps, augments and defends the faith of Christ has a place in Heaven where the blessed enjoy eternal life, it should be hoped that so holy, pious and necessary a cause will be voluntarily assisted by other Christians, because whoever now refuses to provide assistance against the Turks shall be declared an open protector of faithlessness and of the enemies of the Cross of Christ. We therefore resolve that all of us unanimously, through our solemn envoys, shall secure from the Supreme Pontiff with all possible endeavour and diligence and in such manner and form as the said assembly will determine, that His Holiness turn His attention to the fact that the above described collection of tithes is essential for ensuring peace for Christendom, for the defence of the faithful in Christ, and for fighting the enemies of the Cross; and that as the father and shepherd of the faithful He grant from the magnanimity of His goodness and order under strict penalties through His public and authentic bulls the executors nominated to Him and appointed in the most complete form, and dispatched to Him for this purpose, that the said tithes be given, returned and paid in a manner and under conditions submitted to Him in our name; and to end all wars and discord between the princes of the Church who are not parties to the present covenant, and in particular those wars and discord wich might impede in some manner the conclusion of the wars against the Turks and the maintenance of the said peace, or that He send to every province one of the legates, a man of most blameless life, honesty and experience, who is invested with full powers for this purpose, a man who knows and understands the order, speech and customs of such province, who would apply due endeavour and diligence to seeing that the parties in dispute reach an amicable settlement. However, if they should refuse to do so, he should end the continuing differences between them by the power vested in him and decide the dispute in court. His Holiness should also convene the other princes and communities of Italy, admonish them under the threat of divine censure and strict penalties and demand that, being closer neighbours of the Turks than other nations, they should begin building a naval force with the other Christians, contribute to them and provide proportionate

assistance for the honour of God and for the faithful, so that this deed of defence of the faith may more laudably attain the desired end.

[22] Furthermore, so that peace and the present covenant may be inviolably preserved, we have decreed and pledged ourselves that if any of us should be called to the heavenly abode, no heir or successor of his may be allowed to succeed him to the kingdom, principality or dominion, nor may he be admitted thereto unless he has previously pledged in an open letter furnished with his seal and placed at the disposal of any of us as a general guaranty to our assembly that he will observe with inviolable fidelity all what is written above and below in general and in particular.

[23] And if our said assembly or its majority orders, decrees and concludes more than what has been stated above, which will in some manner serve peace and benefit peace and justice as well as the defence of faithful Christians, we shall in truth observe and uphold it all and individually and do what is required and to what we are pledged by the bond of true and sincere fraternity and what is summarized in our present letters in their paragraphs and their contents, in all their points, clauses, articles, sentences and chapters. In witness and confirmation whereof each of our kings and princes has affixed the seal of his majesty to the present letters. Done and acted, etc.

[*Translated by Ivo Dvořák, JUDr., M. A.*]

ТРАКТАТ ОБ УСТАНОВЛЕНИИ МИРА В МИРЕ ХРИСТИАНСКОМ

В<small>о</small> имя Господа нашего Иисуса Христа. Мы, А, В, С, объявляем всем и каждому особо, на вечную память: коль скоро перечитываем мы творения древних летописцев, мы узнаем, что некогда процветало христианство и было одарено людьми и земными благами; царство его так в даль и вширь простиралось, что было в лоне его сто семнадцать пребогатых королевств, а людьми оно было так преисполнено, что на долгие времена подчинило себе великое множество язычников и владело гробом Господним; не было тогда на целом свете народа, который отважился бы тревожить власть христиан. Все мы однако знаем, как ныне христианство разрознено, раздроблено, разбито и лишено всего былого великолепия и блеска. Да и в самом христианстве не так давно настали такие перемены, что если кто из прежних королей, князей или вельмож восстал бы сейчас из мертвых и посетил бы христианские страны, не узнал бы и земли своей собственной. Коварный Магомет, когда почти весь свет был силен святостью веры христианской, смутил сначала малый народ арабов; когда же его первым попыткам не был дан отпор, он вскоре склонил на свою сторону такое множество погибших людей, что подчинил своей власти обширные области Африки и Азии, и подбил их на гнусную измену. Потом препоганейшие турки, которые совсем недавно покорили сначала славную греческую империю, а потом многие христианские страны и королевства, угнали почти бесчисленное множество душ из земель христианских, все берут как добычу, премногие монастыри и большие храмы разрушили и обрекли гибели и бесчисленные другие злодеяния совершили.

О, золотая земля! О, христианство, краса земли, как сгинула твоя слава, как утеряло ты свое блестяще великолепие? Где прежнее горение людей твоих? Где почет, который тебе оказывали все народы, где королевская величественность, где слава? Что пользы было в столь многочисленных победах, коль суждено было, чтобы вскоре тебя влачили в триумфиальном шествии? Что пользы в том, что устояло ты пред силами языческих возждей, коли теперь не можешь отразить нападения соседей? О превратности судьбы! Как быстро меняются империи, как быстро сменяются королевства, как быстро падают власти! Поистине не легко познать причины таких перемен и разорения; ибо скрыты намерения Господни. Поля так же плодородны как некогда, так же плодовиты стада, урожайны виноградники, прибыльны золотые и серебяные рудники; люди разумны, прилежны, мужественны, во многих делах искустны, науки процветают как никогда. Отчего же так пало христианство, что из вышереченных ста семнадцати королевств в лоне христианства осталось лишь шестнадцать? Вероятно за многие грехи хочет наказать нас Господь, что бывало не раз, как читаем мы в Ветхом завете. Поэтому мы полагаем, что нужно тщательно рассудить как исправить то, что ошибочно было и как умилостивить богоугодными делами Господа Бога милосердного, разгневанного грехами нашими. Ибо знаем мы, что Бог справедлив и милосерден к тем, чьи прогрешения он на этом свете карает, что он сам считает людей сыновьями своими, а кого любит, того исправляет и наказывает и через многие злоключения приводит на стезю добродетели; поэтому обращая свои надежды к Господу, за дело которого мы стоим, мы считаем, что не можем сделать ничего более угодного Богу в своем благочестии, ничего более приличествующего нашей чести и ничего более достославного для хвалы нашей, как потрудиться над тем, чтобы между христианами воцарился подлинный, справедливый и длительный мир, единство и любовь и чтобы вера Христова защищена была от свирепейших турок. Для того королевства и княжества нам вверены, чтобы со всей ревностью и усердием мир славился, положение христианства укреплялось, войны против бусурман счастливо велись до конца и границы христианства охранялись и расширялись; а о делах сих все люди, все народы, все короли и князья должны и обязаны радеть с мыслью радостной и охотливой. Ибо если мы называем себя христианами, мы должны заботиться о том, чтобы христианская вера охранялась; а коли мы не хотим быть против Христа, мы обязаны за его веру бороться и при нем стоять. Ведь Дух святой отвергает тех, кто не борется вместе с ним, кто не противостоит (врагу), кто не станет стеной перед домом Израиля. И никто да не отступится от службы Богу, ни ради сладости родины, ни ради великолепных дворцов, ни ради чрезмерного богатства. Ибо нужно служить тому, кто ради нас не побоялся принять смерть на кресте, кто каждому верующему даст в награду родину на небесах, родину истинную, чертоги необозримые, богатство несравненное и жизнь вечную. И потому, хоть и жалка ныне судьба греков и хоть погром Константинополя и прочих земель громко оплакивать следует, нам, коли жаждем мы славы, остается лишь радоваться, что нам дается возможность сохранить честь называться защитниками и охранителями имени христиан. А потому, желая, чтобы такие войны, разбои, беспорядки, пожары и убийства, которыми — увы! — охвачено само христианство уже почти со всех сторон, которые опустошают поля, разрушают города, терзают землю и неисчислимыми бедствиями губят кролевства и княжества, прекратились и были полностью искоренены и в похвальном единстве чтобы воцарилась взаимная любовь и взаимное братство, мы решили на основе наших достоверных знаний, после предшествующего зрелого размышления, призывая милость Духа святого и испросив совета и согласия наших прелатов, князей, вельмож, дворян и докторов божеского и человеческого права создать такой союз единения, мира, братства и согласия, который во имя благочестия и сохранения веры стоял бы непоколебимо и который для нас, наших наследников и будущих наших преемников на вечные времена сохранялся бы в форме, как далее следует.

[1]   Во-первых честью веры католической и словом королевским и княжеским заявляем и обещаем, что от сего часа и дня будем впредь взаимно доказывать и сохранять чистое, настоящее и искреннее братство, что ни при каких несогласиях, жалобах или спорах не будем друг против друга прибегать к оружию и никому не позволим прибегать к нему нашим именем, но будем поддерживать соответственно с содержанием и духом нижеприведенных пунктов один другого против каждого живущего человека, который против нас или против кого-либо из нас попытался бы совершить вражеское не имея на то основанного на праве эдикта.

[2] Во-вторых, что никто из нас не окажет помощи и не даст совета и не вступит в сговор против другого и что ни мы сами, ни через другого или других не будем заниматься происками или на жизнь его покушаться, или вступать в сговор с теми, которые бесправно происки готовить хотели бы, но будем по мере возможности заботиться о сохранении его здоровья, жизни и чести.

[3] В-третьих обещаем и в вышереченном порядке постанавливаем, что если кто из подданных любого из нас один или совместно с другими произведет или произведут какое-либо опустошение, разбой, грабеж или другое злодеяние в королевствах, княжествах или землях другого из нас, то этим названный мир и единство не нарушаются и не расстраиваются, но что такие злодеи будут обязаны пополнить изъян, если не по доброй воле, то через суд по требованию того в области юрисдикции которого они проживают или на территории которого они будут уличены как преступники: из их имущества возместиться ущерб ими причиненный, а они сами будут соответственно характеру преступления и другим обстоятельствам надлежаще наказаны; тех же преступников, которые суду не подчинятся, будут их государи по месту жительства или по месту совершения преступления обязаны и должны преследовать и губить, не ожидая пока начнет другой. Если же кто из нас, в чьей области преступник проживает или на территории кого будет преступление совершено и преступник задержан, не выполнит вышереченные (принципы) и пренебрежет (ими), то, поелику его и преступника по праву должна постичь одинаковая кара, тот, кому нанесена обида или ущерб, может такого из нас перед нижереченным парламентом или консисторией преследовать по суду и жалобу на него подать.

[4] В-четвертых постанавливаем, что если кто или некоторые, вне сего договора, любви и братства нашего стоящие не претерпев от нас обиды и не будучи провокированы, против кого-либо из нас войну начали или начать ее замышляли (чего опасаться не надо, коли наша дружба и любовь будут нерушимы), то наше нижереченное собрание вышлет тогда от имени всех участников договора сего и на наш общий счет, даже если подвергшийся нападению друг того и не просит, своих достойных послов для разрешения спора и востановления мира в место удобное для сторон, чтобы они там, в присутствии спорящих сторон или их послов, снабженных полномочиями, со всем усердием и верностью старались склонить спорящие стороны к согласию и миру путем дружеским, если это возможно, или уговорить их избрать арбитров либо домагаться права у соотвествующего судьи, парламента или консистории, в порядке ниже указанном. Если же из-за того или по вине того, кто начал войну, нельзя было восстановить мир и единство одним из вышереченных способов, то тогда мы все прочие единодушным и согласным решением поможем подвергшемуся нападению и защищаемому другу нашему в его обороне из десятины наших королевств и из доходов, прибыли и поступлений подданных наших, которые они в среднем в течение трех дней расходуют из года в год на нужды своего дома и домохозяйства, в таком размере и на такой срок, как решит и постановит сие собрание наше или его большинство в качестве соразмерного и надлежащего для того, чтобы наш нападению подвергшийся друг добился мира.

[5] А для того, чтобы пресекать военные раздоры, коли одно помышление о них причиняет страдания тем, кого они постигают, и для упрочнения мира и среди прочих верных Христу, которые не участвуют в нашем договоре, мы постановляем и приказываем, чтобы в случае возникновения распрей и войн между другими, в наше братство не входящими христианскими князьями и магнатами, наше ниже-реченное собрание от нашего имени и на наши общие средства выслало послов, чтобы они по возможности дружески или в порядке права, как указано выше, установили между спорящими сторонами согласие; если же обе стороны или одна из них не хотели бы или не хотела бы прийти к согласию в этом порядке и раздоры и войну прекратить, то тогда тот, кто войну начал или от войны отказаться не хочет, будет приведен в подчинение способами и формами, в предстоящей статье указанными.

[6] Далее постановляем, что те, кто отважится любым способом нарушать наш нынешний мир, не смеют и не могут приниматься, наниматься на службу, пользоваться защитой и поддержкой или под каким-либо выисканным предлогом получать благодеяния или дары ни в одном из наших королевств, княжеств, владений, территорий и областей, замков, городов, сел или крепостей; невзирая ни на какие охранные грамоты, они будут заключаться в тюрьмы, задерживаться и наказываться как нарушители общего мира соответственно характеру преступления или вины, каждый как того заслуживает.

[7] Кроме того постановляем и настоящим обязуем наших слуг и подданных, всех и каждого особливо, чтобы они никогда — сообща или в отдельности — не принимали под свою охрану и защиту какого-либо человека и ему никоим образом не предоставляли и не выдавали общей или особой охранной грамоты, не оговорив особо и нарочито, что охранная грамота или гарантия не будут того, кому они выданы, защищать и охранять от мер по нашему нынешнему миру, чтобы в случае, если он будет обвинен, подозреваем в нарушении мира или привлечен к ответственности за нарушение мира, можно было с ним беспрепятственно поступать по справедливости, как указано выше.

[8] Кто же умышленно вступит в сговор с нарушителем нынешнего мира и ему под любым выисканным предлогом либо совет даст, либо окажет помощь, или благодеяние, либо примет или его самого будет охранять или защищать, либо выдать ему охранную грамоту против нашего настоящего единения отважится, того да постигнет такая же кара, как и злодея.

[9] Понеже забота о мире немыслима без справедливости, справедливость без нее, ибо из справедливости мир родится и сохраняется и понеже мы и подданные наши не можем без справедливости в мире

пребывать, мы связываем справедливость с делом мира; но поелику закон, который был написан о судопроизводстве, в последующее время подвергся многим изменениям и дело дошло до того, что он постепенно потерял значение вовсе, а практика толкованием облекла его в совершенно иную форму, мы считаем судебные правила совершенно перепутанными и полагаем, что соответственно с обычаями, обыкновениями и условиями нового времени и наших разных стран, королевств и княжеств следует ввести новые, из лона природы почерпнутые правила и с новыми злодеяниями бороться новыми средствами, которыми добродетельные люди вознаграждались бы, а преступники молотом наказаний неустанно уничтожались. А чтобы отдельные дела по порядку рассматривать, решили мы прежде всего учредить одну общую консисторию, которая от имени всех нас и всего нашего собрания заседала бы в месте, где само собрание как раз пребывает, и из нее как из источника, текли бы ручьи справедливости во все стороны. А суд этот будет учрежден соответственно с тем, как наше нижереченное собрание или его большинство постановит и решит о числе лиц и их квалификации и о правилах судоговорения.

[10] А чтобы в этом суде споры заканчивались, а не тянулись до бесконечности, постанавливаем, чтобы по характеру спора судья сам и его заседатели для спорящих сторон производство вели и правду находили просто и ясно без формальностей судебной волокиты, отказавшись от отговорок и излишних отсрочек.

[11] Далее постанавливаем, чтобы в случаях, когда между нами королями и князьями и другими участниками нашего договора вновь возникнут какие-либо споры и распри, был один перед другим обязан и должен в суде нашем по праву ответ держать и с ним спор вести и соблюдать при этом постановления, решения и распоряжения, которые представители наши или их большинство в самом собрании, как указано выше, вынесут или издадут.

[12] Далее постановляем, что наше собрание должно иметь полную и неограниченную свободу соответствующими грамотами, взаимно выданными и принятыми, любого христианского короля, князя или магната, которые пока еще не входят в это единение, в настоящий наш мир, единение любви и братства, принимать и от имени нашего так, словно мы сами это делали, обязываться, а также обязательства взаимной дружбы принимать, с тем только добавлением, что немедля, как только такое принятие совершено будет, само собрание нас всех о том уведомит, чтобы мы с принятым к нам могли с братской любовью обращаться как приличествует.

[13] Поелику это единение, согласие и любовь были заключены и учреждаются прежде всего во славу и честь величия божия, святой церкви римской и веры католической и для того, чтобы как можно скорее тем верным Христу, что угнетаются князем турок, самым лютым врагом имени христиан, помощь

оказать, мы вышереченные короли и князья обещаем и клянемся Господу нашему Иисусу Христу, его преславной матери Деве Марии и святой церкви римской, что будем охранять и защищать веру христианскую и всех притесняемых верующих от мерзейшего князя турок взаимно объединенными силами и средствами, которые будут соразмерно установлены и объявлены, для обретения и обеспечения коих внесем и отдадим, коли в этом нужда будет, все десятины, которые уплачиваются церквам, как и церковным и духовным лицам в наших королевствах, княжествах и владениях вместе с названными поступлениями, прибылями и доходами нашими и наших подданных, которые, как выше указано, в отдельные года за три дня расходуются, и не перестанем преследовать врага, если это будет признано полезным союзом нашим, до тех пор пока он не будет изгнан с территории христиан или пока по совместному решению не будет постановлено заключить мир, который может быть заключен лишь при условии, что безопасность соседних христиан будет считаться обеспеченной.

[14] Кроме того, ибо надо наперед умело и тщательно того избегать, что наконец может в несчастье ввергнуть, постановляем мы, что общим решеением всего нашего собрания или большинства его устанавливается, когда пригодно будет напасть на неприятеля или какими сухопутными и морскими силами вестись война должна и под началом каких полководцев, какие машины или военные средства должны быть использованы, в каком месте должны собраться все сухопутные войска, которые далее в поход на турок отправятся. Далее в каком порядке можно было бы приобретать за соответственные цены провиант и расквартирование в городах, селах и других подходящих местах. Далее, в каком порядке была бы введена единая монета, чтобы воины в походе, на постое и при возвращении не имели затруднений. Далее да будет общим решением установлено в зависимости от того, как будет признано и положено, что в будущем поможет больше вере христианской и больше безопасности верующих, кому и что надо передать в том случае, если что-нибудь удастся вырвать из рук или из под власти врага, так, чтобы враг нерадением или неспособностью держателей снова ободренный, не причинил верующим новых бед, хуже предшествующих.

[15] Кроме того постанавливаем, чтобы каждый из нас, как только будет принято решение, незамедлительно приступил к вышереченному сбору денег в своем королевстве, княжестве и владениях, в порядке или форме, которые будут определены самим собранием или большинством его для той цели, чтобы богоугодное дело сие немедля осуществлялось и верным во Христе была оказана помощь.

[16] Далее. Чтобы надлежаще было выполнено выше и ниже написанное, все вместе и особливо, мы обязуемся и обещаем в вышереченном порядке, чтобы каждый из нас к ближайшему следующему воскресенью "Реминисцере" года тысяча пятьсот шестьдесят четвертого от рождения Господа, имел в городе

Базеле в Германии своих послов, мужей достойных и весьма уважаемых, снабженных широчайшими полномочиями и своею печатью, которые там все постоянно заседали бы в течение непосредственно следующих пяти лет и от нашего имени и от имени прочих членов или же тех, которые должны быть приняты в союз, создали, образовали и составляли корпорацию, единение или надлежащую коллегию. А по истечении этого пятилетия собрания базельского пусть то же собрание в течение непосредственно следующего пятилетия находится в городе Н. во Франции, а в течение третьего пятилетия — в городе Н. в Италии происходить и устраиваться будет, при тех же условиях и обстоятельствах, как выше принято и постановлено о Базеле, чтобы потом всегда по истечении пяти лет собрание меняло свое местопребывание до того времени, когда само собрание или его большинство постановит и решит иначе. Собрание да будет иметь один собственный и особый совет, председателем которого да будет Н., как отец и голова, а мы, прочие короли и князья будем его членами. Да будет названная коллегия иметь над нами всеми и подданными нашими, как и над теми, кто добровольно подчинится, юрисдикцию спорную и неспорную вместе с чистыми и смешанными полномочиями в зависимости от того, как решит и установит сие собрание или его большинство. Наконец пусть собрание имеет свой герб, печать и общую казну и общественный архив, синдика, фискала, чиновников и все прочие права разрешенной и исправной корпорации свойственные и принадлежащие.

[17] А чтобы каждой стране сохранялись нерушимые права ее, постанавливаем, чтобы во главу высших учреждений собрания были в каждой нации, где собрание находится, назначаемы те, кто в нации этой родились, кто знают и понимают ее нравы и обычаи.

[18] Наконец, чтобы нашему собранию хватало средств на расходы и издержки, необходимые и полезные для сохранения мира, отправления правосудия, посылке послов и представителей в разные стороны и на другие надобности, обещаем и обязуемся, что каждый из нас без дальнейшего промедления пошлет и передаст в общественный архив сборщикам и совету упомянутого собрания десятую долю всех денег, которые должны быть собраны им или от его имени с десятков, трехдневных доходов или прибылей, как было указано выше, в срок, который само собрание или его большинство установит. А если кто того не учинит, то синдик или фискальный прокурор настоящего собрания может и должен тотчас же на него жалобу в парламент или в суд подать и через суд взыскать деньги с проторями и процентами, как и нас прочих, связанных присягой вере принесенной, увещевать и напоминать нам, чтобы мы эти деньги, возмещение проторей и проценты от него и подданных взыскивали военной силой, чтобы они, как выше сказано, были обращены на общие нужды собрания.

[19] Далее объявляем и устанавливаем, чтобы в этом собрании имели и составляли один голос мы, король Франции, вместе с прочими королями и князьями Галлии, затем второй — мы, короли и князья

Германской империи, а третий мы, дож венецианский с князьями и городскими общинами Италии. А если бы к этому нашему единению, дружбе и братству присоединится король Кастилии или другие короли и князья нации гишпанской, то и они сами подобно нам будут иметь в собрании, корпорации и коллегии один голос. Если же между представителями королей и князей одной и той же нации по какому-либо делу возникнут и будут высказаны противоречивые взгляды, то постанавливается, чтобы впредь имело силу — словно бы от самой нации единодушным соглашением решено и указано — то, что было признано и постановлено большинством. Если же будет равенство голосов, то преимущество должны иметь те представители, которые по сравнению с другими отличаются большими заслугами и достойностью своих господ, ими представляемых. А коли равны они и в заслугах и достоинстве, то да будет предоставлено выбору остальных наций, в этом соглашении объединенных, к какой из сторон они присоединятся.

[20]   А чтобы устранить любые сомнения, постанавливается, что в том случае, когда кто-либо из наших королей или князей пошлет на названное собрание нескольких представителей, все они будут иметь только один голос, а именно голос пославшего их, в его национальной курии названного собрания.

[21]   Далее — поелику Писание говорит о том, что для того, кто поможет вере Христовой или ее размножит или охранит, уготовано место на небесах, где блаженство вечное, надо надеяться, что к делу столь святому, столь богоугодному и столь необходимому и все прочие христиане добровольно руку приложат, ибо тот, кто сейчас откажется предоставить помощь против турок, будет объявлен явным защитником безбожия и врагом креста Христова. А потому постанавливаем, что мы все единодушно через посредство наших достойных послов, всеми нам доступными стараниями, и заботами, и способами, и формами, установленными названным собранием, обеспечим у высшего пастыря, чтобы Его Святейшество обратило внимание на то, что вышереченный сбор десятины требуется для обеспечения мира христиан, для защиты верных Христу и для борьбы против врагов креста; и чтобы он, как отец и пастырь верующих, в неисчерпаемой доброте своей разрешил и приказал под угрозой строгого наказания, в своих общих и аутентичных торжественных грамотах исполнителям, которые ему будут названы и для этой цели совершеннейшей формой назначены и посланы, названную десятину взымать, принимать и выплачивать в порядке и в соответствии с условиями, которые будут от нашего имени ему предложены; чтобы он быстро пресек все войны и раздоры между духовными князьями, которые не являются участниками настоящего договора, а прежде всего те, которые как-либо могли бы быть препятствием окончания войн против турок и сохранения названного мира, или же чтобы он в каждую страну послал кого-либо из легатов, мужа жизни добропорядочной, честного и опытного, который порядки, речь и обычаи этой страны знает и понимает, чтобы он надлежащими старанием и прилежанием способствовал, чтобы спорящие стороны дружески договорились. Если же они так учинить не захотели бы, то пусть он в силу данного ему поручения продолжающимся раздорам положит конец

и вынесет решение как судья. И пусть Его Святейшество созовет прочих князей и города Италии и под божественными санкциями и жестокими наказаниями увещает и потребует, чтобы они, как ближайшие по сравнению с прочими нациями соседи турок, приступили к созданию морского флота вместе с прочими христианами и оказывали им содействие и вносили посильную лепту во славу и честь божью и на защиту верующих, чтобы дело защиты веры тем самым достигло заслуживающей похвалы и чаятельной цели.

[22] Кроме того, чтобы мир и это соглашение нерушимыми остались, мы решили и обещаем, что в том случае, если кто-либо из нас будет отозван в царство небесное, не будет никому из его наследников или преемников разрешено принять королевство, княжество или владение и не может он быть к тому допущен, прежде чем не даст обещания своей открытой печатью снабженной грамотой и как общее ручательство нашему собранию любому из нас переданной, что он сам будет все вместе и особливо выше и ниже описанное соблюдать с верностью непоколебимой.

[23] А ежели наше названное собрание или его большинство распорядится, решит или заключит еще что-либо другое кроме вышереченного, что любым путем будет служить миру и содействовать миру и справедливости, как и защите верных христиан, то все это в целом и в отдельности мы будем соблюдать и подлинно хранить, как совершать и то, чего требуют и к чему обязывают узы истинного и искреннего братства и что изложено в нашей настоящей грамоте по статьям и в их содержании во всех пунктах, клаузулах, абзацах, фразах и главах. В свидетельство и утверждение чего каждый король и князь приложил к настоящей грамоте свою владетельскую печать. Дано и обсуждено и т.д.

[*Перевод Л. П. Можанской и Е. В. Тарабрина*]

TRAITÉ DESTINÉ À ÉTABLIR LA PAIX DANS TOUTE LA CHRÉTIENTÉ

Au nom de notre Seigneur Jésus Christ. Nous A. B. C. faisons connaître à tous ensemble et à chacun en particulier pour qu'ils en gardent la mémoire perpétuelle: lorsque nous lisons les écrits des anciens historiens, nous découvrons que la Chrétienté, riche en hommes et en biens, se trouvait jadis dans tout son épanouissement, que telle était son étendue en longueur et en largeur qu'elle finit par englober dans son sein cent dix-sept royaumes considérables; et qu'elle donna naissance à une telle multitude d'hommes qu'elle parvint à s'emparer pour longtemps d'une grande partie des pays païens, y compris le Sépulcre de notre Seigneur. Et il n'y eut aucun peuple alors dans le monde entier qui osât attaquer la puissance des chrétiens. Or nous savons tous combien de nos jours la Chrétienté est brisée, détruite, misérable et dépouillée de son éclat et de sa splendeur d'auparavant. Car de tels changements sont survenus depuis peu de temps au sein même de la Chrétienté que si quelque roi, prince ou seigneur du passé réssuscitait et visitait les pays chrétiens, il ne reconnaîtrait même pas son propre pays. En effet, alors que le monde presque entier trouvait sa grandeur dans la sainteté de la religion chrétienne, l'astucieux Mahomet commença par séduire le petit peuple arabe. Mais comme on avait négligé de s'opposer à ses premières tentatives, il ne tarda pas à gagner peu à peu une telle multitude de gens égarés qu'il finit par conquérir les parties les plus vastes de l'Afrique et de l'Asie qu'il entraîna à la plus abominable trahison. Pour finir, les ignobles Turcs, qui ces derniers temps assujettirent d'abord le glorieux Empire grec, ensuite un grand nombre de provinces et royaumes chrétiens, enlevèrent des âmes en nombre presque infini au domaine de la Chrétienté; emportant tout comme leur butin, ils démolirent ou amenèrent à l'état de ruine beaucoup de monastères et magnifiques temples de Dieu et commirent et perpétrèrent une quantité infinie d'autres maux.

Ô Royaume d'or! Ô Chrétienté, parure des nations, comment tout honneur a-t-il pu te quitter, comment tes plus riantes couleurs ont-elles pu s'évanouir? Qu'est devenue cette belle vigueur de tes hommes? Où est la vénération dont tu jouissait auprès de tous les peuples, où ta royale majesté, où ta gloire? A quoi t'auront servi tant de victoires si tu devais si tôt figurer en vaincue dans le cortège triomphal? A quoi bon avoir résisté à la puissance de chefs païens si tu n'as plus la force à présent de repousser les attaques de tes voisins? Hélas, mauvaise fortune, hélas, destins changeants! Combien vite passent les souverainetés, combien vite se transforment les royaumes, combien vite s'effondrent les pouvoirs. Discerner la cause d'un tel changement et d'une telle ruine n'est pas facile, car les desseins de Dieu sont impénétrables. Comme autrefois, les champs ne sont pas moins fertiles qu'ils ne l'étaient jadis, les troupeaux pas moins féconds, les vendanges pas moins belles, les mines d'or et d'argent pas moins lucratives, les hommes sont doués de raison, industrieux, magnanimes, experts en bien des choses, les belles-lettres fleurissent comme jamais auparavant. Qu'est-ce donc qui a humilié la Chrétienté qu'au lieu de cent dix-sept royaumes, comme il a été dit, ils n'en sont plus dans son giron que seize? Sans doute s'agit-il de nombreux péchés que Dieu veut châtier, comme il le fit fréquemment jadis ainsi que nous le lisons dans l'Ancien Testament. C'est pourquoi il nous semble qu'il faut considérer attentivement cet état de choses afin d'amender les erreurs, s'il en a été commis et d'apaiser par des actes de piété la majesté divine qui de toute évidence a été offensée par quelque injustice. Mais nous savons que Dieu use de justice et de miséricorde avec ses fils, qu'il corrige et châtie ceux qu'il aime et, par le long chemin des adversités, les induit aux œuvres de la vertu. C'est pourquoi plaçant notre espérance dans le Seigneur et dans sa juste cause, nous tenons pour certain que nous ne pourrons rien faire de plus convenable à notre sainteté, de plus conforme à notre probité, de plus digne de notre gloire, que de nous efforcer d'établir entre les chrétiens paix véritable, pure et solide, ainsi qu'union et charité pour que la foi chrétienne soit défendue contre l'abominable Turc. Car c'est pour cela que nous ont été confiés les royaumes et les principautés, afin que nous honorions la paix de tout le zèle et tous les soins possibles, que la situation de la Chrétienté soit soutenue, les guerres contre les infidèles menées à bonne fin et le territoire de la Chrétienté protégé et agrandi. C'est à cette fin que tous les peuples, toutes les nations, tous les rois et princes se doivent et sont tenus d'employer leurs efforts d'un cœur joyeux et résolu. Puisque nous nous disons chrétiens, nous sommes tenus de veiller à la défense de la foi chrétienne et si nous ne voulons pas nous dresser contre le Christ, nous sommes obligés de combattre pour sa foi et de nous tenir à ses côtés. Car le Saint-Esprit maudit ceux qui ne combattent pas à ses côtés, qui ne font pas face à l'ennemi et ne se placent pas, comme un mur, devant la maison d'Israël. Ni la douceur du pays natal, ni les palais magnifiques, ni de grandes richesses ne sauraient détourner qui que ce fût du service de Dieu. Il faut servir qui n'a pas craint de subir pour nous la mort sur la croix, qui donnera en récompense à chaque croyant la patrie céleste, notre vraie patrie, où sont d'immenses demeures, d'incomparables richesses et la vie éternelle. Oui, pour lamentable que soit aujourd'hui le sort des Grecs et malgré notre grande affliction du désastre de Constantinople et d'autres pays, nous devons souhaiter l'occasion qui puisse nous réserver l'honneur d'être appelés les défenseurs et les sauveurs du nom chrétien. C'est pourquoi, par le désir de voir cesser les guerres, pillages, désordres, incendies et massacres qui-comme nous l'avons, hélas, déjà dit-ont investi presque de toutes parts la Chrétienté même, dépeuplant les champs, pillant les villes, saccageant les provinces, écrasant royaumes et principautés de malheurs sans nombre, désireux donc que tant de méfaits prennent fin et soient extirpés en profondeur, afin qu'on revienne à l'état convenable de charité mutuelle et de fraternité par l'union si désirable, nous, instruits à bonne source, après mûre délibération, ayant invoqué sur notre projet la grâce du Saint-Esprit, appelé en conseil et approbation nos prélats, princes, seigneurs, gentilshommes et docteurs en droit divin et humain — nous avons décidé de sceller dans la forme qui suit un pacte établissant *union, paix, fraternité et concorde inébranlables, pour la vénération de Dieu et la sauvegarde de la foi à jamais et à perpétuité, pour nous, nos héritiers et nos successeurs à venir.*

[1°]   En premier lieu, sur l'honneur de la foi catholique et sur notre parole de roi et de prince nous faisons déclaration et promesse de montrer et d'observer l'un envers l'autre de cette heure et de ce jour, pure, véritable et sincère fraternité, de ne pas recourir aux armes l'un contre l'autre, quelle que soit la nature de nos différends, discussions ou griefs, et de ne pas permettre à qui que ce soit d'y avoir recours en notre nom, mais bien plutôt de nous prêter assistance réciproque conformément au texte et à l'esprit des dispositions ci-dessous, contre tout homme vivant qui entreprendrait de nous attaquer ou d'attaquer l'un de nous de fait et sans édit légitime.

[2°]   En second lieu, nous promettons qu'aucun de nous n'apportera aide ou conseil, ni ne complotera contre la personne d'un autre parmi nous et que ni nous-mêmes ni par l'intermédiaire d'un autre ne machïnerons aucun complot ou attentat contre la personne d'un autre ou d'autres, mais que nous veillerons, au contraire, à maintenir sa santé, sa vie et son honneur selon notre pouvoir.

[3°]   En troisième lieu, nous garantissons, comme ci-dessus dit, que si l'un ou plusieurs des sujets de l'un d'entre nous commet ou commettent dévastations, pillages, rapines, incendies ou toute sorte de méfaits dans les royaumes, principautés ou terres de l'un de nous, la paix et l'union n'en seront ni troublées ni rompues, mais que les malfaiteurs seront amenés à réparer les dommages. S'il est impossible d'obtenir satisfaction à l'amiable, ils seront traduits en justice par celui dans la juridiction duquel les coupables ont leur résidence, ou sur le territoire duquel le crime a été constaté, de façon que le dommage commis soit réparé par ses auteurs à leurs dépens, et eux-mêmes châtiés à proportion du délit. Si les malfaiteurs bravent le tribunal, leur seigneur, quel qu'il soit, tant au lieu de leur résidence qu'à celui de leur délit, sans que l'un s'en remette à l'autre, sera tenu et obligé de les poursuivre et mettre hors d'état de nuire en tant que malfaiteurs. Que si l'un d'entre nous sous l'autorité duquel réside le coupable ou bien sur le territoire duquel le délit a été commis et le coupable appréhendé, a négligé d'appliquer les précédentes dispositions ou remis à le faire, il soit passible d'une sanction égale à celle infligée au coupable. La victime de l'injustice ou du dommage aura le droit de poursuivre et citer en justice celui d'entre nous devant le Parlement ou Consistoire prévu plus loin.

[4°] En quatrième lieu, s'il arrivait que quelqu'un ou quelques-uns, ne faisant pas partie de notre convention, charité et fraternité, fît la guerre ou entreprît de la faire à l'un d'entre nous et cela sans molestations ou provocations de notre côté ce qui n'est absolument pas à craindre, aussi longtemps que durera cette amitié et charité, notre Assemblée prévue plus loin, au nom de tous les signataires du pacte — même si l'allié attaqué ne nous a pas fait appel — enverra à frais communs et solennellement, en vue d'aplanir le différend et de ménager la paix, une délégation qui devra se transporter au plus vite en un endroit commode aux deux parties; et là, en présence des parties en litige ou de leurs représentants munis de pleins pouvoirs, nos délégués feront tout effort et diligence pour ramener paix et concorde entre les adversaires, si possible par voie amicale; sinon ils les engageront à choisir des arbitres ou à plaider devant la juridiction compétente ou devant le Parlement ou Consistoire prévu ci-dessous. Si l'assaillant faisant défaut en justice, paix et union ne peuvent pas être rétablies par l'un des moyens susdits, nous tous sans exception, en application d'une décision unanime et prise en parfait accord, viendrons au secours de notre allié, qu'il soit attaqué ou qu'il se défende, en lui attribuant le produit de dîmes provenant de nos royaumes ainsi que de la part des revenus, bénéfices et gains calculés proportionnellement par nos sujets à l'entretien de leur maison et ménage pendant trois jours par an chaque année. Le montant et la durée en auront été appréciés et fixés par notre Assemblée ou par sa majorité de façon convenable et avantageuse au rétablissement de la paix pour notre allié attaqué.

[5°] Afin que soient davantage encore écartées les divisions causées par les guerres dont la seule perspective suffit à susciter les souffrances de ceux qui se les infligent réciproquement, afin que la paix règne entre les autres fidèles du Christ étrangers à notre pacte, nous voulons et disposons, s'il survenait des différends ou la guerre entre d'autres princes ou seigneurs chrétiens non incorporés à notre fraternité, que notre Assemblée, mentionnée ci-dessous, par l'entremise d'une délégation envoyée à frais communs ramène la concorde entre les adversaires, si possible par procédure amicale, ou par voie de justice comme prévu ci-dessus; si les deux parties — ou l'une d'elles — ne voulaient pas accepter l'accord et cesser les combats et les guerres, que celui qui a commencé la guerre ou celui qui ne veut pas la cesser y soit contraint par les moyens et règlements suscrits à l'article précédent.

[6°] De même nous voulons que quiconque oserait de quelque manière troubler l'état de paix institué présentement, ne doive ni ne puisse être recueilli, engagé, protégé, aidé ni ne doive jouir d'une faveur sous un quelconque prétexte dans aucun de nos royaumes, principautés, domaines, territoires et circonscriptions, châteaux forts et villes, communes ou forteresses. Qui plus est, aucun sauf-conduit ne pourra faire obstacle à l'arrestation, saisie et châtiment de ces personnes, comme profanateurs de la paix générale, selon la sanction encourue par la nature de leur crime ou délit.

[7°] En outre nous stipulons et nous enjoignons par les présentes à tous nos fonctionnaires et sujets et à chacun d'eux, de n'accorder aide et protection à personne — tant en commun qu'en particulier — et de ne délivrer de sauf-conduit, général ou particulier, que sous réserve expresse que ce sauf-conduit ou cette protection ne sauraient prémunir celui à qui ils auront été donnés, contre les mesures prises en vue de protéger et défendre la présente paix. Mais celui qui aura été suspecté, accusé ou convaincu d'enfreindre la paix, pourra, sans que rien s'y oppose, être poursuivi par moyens de justice, ainsi qu'il est prévu plus haut.

[8°] Celui qui s'associerait sciemment avec un perturbateur de la présente paix, ou sous quelque prétexte spécieux lui apporterait appui, aide et conseil, ou oserait l'accueillir ou protéger ou oserait lui délivrer un sauf-conduit contre notre présente union, connaîtra le même châtiment que le coupable.

[9°] Cependant, le culte de la paix ne pouvant exister sans la justice, ni la justice sans la paix, puisque c'est de la justice que la paix prend naissance et garde vie, que nous et nos sujets ne pourrions vivre en paix sans la justice, ainsi associons-nous la justice à la cause de la paix. Or, les règlements de la procédure judiciaire ayant subi, au cours des temps, beaucoup d'altérations, en sont, peu à peu, arrivés à se dégrader tout à fait, d'où vient qu'à l'interprétation, la pratique leur a donné un visage tout différent; c'est pourquoi, considérant le désordre complet dans lequel sont tombés lesdits règlements, nous estimons qu'il convient, compte tenu des coutumes, usages et habitudes de notre époque et des provinces, royaumes et principautés très différents, de faire sortir du sein de la nature un droit nouveau, d'adopter, contre des abus nouveaux, de nouveaux remèdes, grâce auxquels on pourrait récompenser les gens de bien et frapper sans arrêt les coupables du marteau des châtiments. Pour mettre de l'ordre dans la matière, nous prévoyons, pour commencer, un Consistoire général qui se tienne, au nom de nous tous et de notre Assemblée, dans le lieu qui sera le siège temporaire de l'Assemblée elle-même. De ce Consistoire, comme d'une fontaine, les ruisseaux de la justice couleraient de toutes parts. Pour ce qui est du nombre et des titres des membres de cette Cour ainsi que de ses statuts, cette

Cour sera organisée conformément aux conclusions et aux décisions de l'Assemblée prévue ci-dessous ou de sa majorité.

[10°]   Pour que les procès plaidés devant cette Cour connaissent un terme et ne traînent pas à l'infini, nous entendons que le juge et ses assesseurs, selon que l'aura requis la nature du litige, procèdent et fassent justice aux plaideurs d'une manière simple et claire, sans formules ni apparat, en proscrivant tous subterfuges et ajournements dilatoires.

[11°]   Arrêtons, en outre, au cas où de nouvelles querelles et divergences venaient à s'élever entre nous, rois et princes, et d'autres parties à notre pacte, que l'un et l'autre soit obligé et tenu de comparaître et plaider dans les formes devant notre dite Cour, en observant les statuts, décrets et règlements faits et établis par nos envoyés et représentants ou par la majorité de l'Assemblée, comme ci-dessus.

[12°]   De même voulons aussi que notre Assemblée puisse avoir libre et entière faculté de recevoir dans notre présente paix, union, charité et fraternité tous rois, princes et seigneurs chrétiens qui, pour le moment, ne sont pas encore membres de notre union; en outre, de prendre et recevoir, en notre nom — au moyen de lettres appropriées délivrées et reçues de part et d'autre — des engagements réciproques, ainsi que nous-mêmes l'avons fait, étant stipulé, en outre, qu'après l'adhésion, l'Assemblée nous en informera sans retard, afin que nous soyons en mesure et moyens de recevoir les nouveaux associés, comme il convient, d'une affection fraternelle.

[13°]   Et comme cette union, entente et charité a été conclue et constituée avant tout pour la gloire et l'honneur de la majesté divine, de la Sainte Eglise romaine et de la foi catholique et pour qu'il soit possible de porter le plus prompt secours possible aux fidèles du Christ opprimés par le prince des Turcs, l'ennemi le plus acharné du nom chrétien, nous, rois et princes ci-dessus nommés, promettons — prenant à témoin Notre Seigneur Jésus Christ, la Vierge Marie, sa très glorieuse Mère, et la Sainte Eglise romaine — de défendre et protéger la foi chrétienne et tous les fidèles accablés par le très abominable prince des Turcs, mettant en commun nos forces et moyens, fixés et déclarés à proportion. Pour nous les procurer et les rassembler, nous verserons et donnerons toutes les dîmes levées dans nos royaumes, principautés et domaines au profit des églises, des ecclésiastiques et des religieux; on y joindra nos revenus, gains et profits et ceux de nos sujets, représentant, comme dit ci-dessus, trois journées de dépense par an que nous payerons et donnerons aussi longtemps qu'il sera nécessaire. Nous ne cesserons pas de poursuivre l'ennemi, si notre Assemblée le juge utile, tant qu'il n'aura pas été chassé du territoire chrétien, ou bien qu'en vertu d'une résolution prise en commun, nous ne serons pas convenus de faire la paix; laquelle ne devra être signée, à moins qu'on n'ait jugé qu'elle garantissait la sécurité des chrétiens avoisinants.

[14°] En outre, comme il faut veiller à tout avec habilité, zèle et diligence, avant que la mauvaise fortune n'en vienne à perdre l'imprudent, nous décidons que sera fixé par une résolution commune de notre Assemblée unanime ou de sa majorité, quel moment sera opportun pour attaquer l'ennemi, avec quelles forces terrestres et navales la guerre devra être menée, quels chefs d'armée doivent les conduire, quelles machines et matériel de guerre être utilisés, en quel lieu se rassembler toutes les forces terrestres pour marcher contre les Turcs. Egalement, comment pouvoir se ravitailler à de justes prix, comment assurer le logement dans les cités, villes et autres lieux appropriés. Egalement, comment introduire une monnaie unique pour l'armée afin que les soldats n'éprouvent pas de difficultés en marche, en garnison ou à leur retour. De même, une résolution prise en commun devra dire à qui attribuer le territoire qu'on aura trouvé le moyen d'arracher des mains ou du pouvoir de l'ennemi, selon ce qu'on aura reconnu et jugé convenir le mieux aux intérêts de la religion chrétienne et à la sécurité future des fidèles, afin d'éviter que l'ennemi, encouragé à récidiver par la négligence ou par la faiblesse des possesseurs, ne cause aux fidèles des dommages pires qu'auparavant.

[15°] En outre, voulons qu'après conclusion de notre pacte, chacun de nous procède sans tarder à la levée des subsides, comme prévu ci-dessus, dans son royaume, sa principauté ou son domaine, selon les formes et règlements prévus à cet effet par l'Assemblée elle-même ou par sa majorité, afin que cette tâche divine soit exécutée sans délai, et les fidèles du Christ secourus.

[16°] De même, afin que tout ce qui précède et ce qui suit, soit exécuté en général et en particulier, chacun de nous prend engagement et fait promesse, ainsi qu'il est dit plus haut, le dimanche de *Reminiscere* le plus proche de l'an mil quatre cent soixante quatre de la naissance du Seigneur, d'envoyer dans la ville de Bâle en Germanie ses représentants choisis parmi des hommes remarquables et de grande valeur, munis de pouvoirs les plus étendus, revêtus de son sceau. Ils y siègeront en permanence les cinq années suivant immédiatement et formeront, constitueront et représenteront, en notre nom ainsi qu'au nom des autres membres et de ceux qui pourront le devenir, véritablement corps, communauté et corporation. Le quinquennat de cette Assemblée à Bâle une fois écoulé, la même Assemblée se tiendra pendant un deuxième quinquennat sans intervalle ni interruption dans la ville de N. en France, et pendant un troisième quinquennat dans la ville de N. en Italie; elle y observera les mêmes règles et les clauses qui auront été retenues pour sages et appliquées précédemment à Bâle; de façon que de ville en ville et d'un quinquennat à l'autre, un circuit soit formé jusqu'au jour où soit l'Assemblée, soit sa majorité jugera qu'il convient de prendre d'autres règlements et dispositions. L'Assemblée, en tant que telle, aura un seul Conseil, en propre et spécial, un seul président, N., son père et son chef, tandis que nous autres, les rois et les princes de la Chrétienté, en serons les membres. Sur nous tous, sur nos sujets et sur ceux qui seraient admis par la suite, ladite corporation exercera aussi juridiction, tant gracieuse que contentieuse et disposera du droit absolu et du droit mixte, selon les dispositions qu'aura décrétées et fixées la même Assemblée ou sa majorité. Enfin, elle aura en propre ses armes, son sceau, son trésor commun, ses archives publiques, un syndic, un procurateur fiscal, des fonctionnaires, ainsi que tous les autres droits concernant et intéressant en quelque manière une union conforme au droit et à la justice.

[17°] Afin que les droits de chaque pays soient conservés intacts, nous stipulons qu'on désignera pour les charges supérieures de l'Assemblée, dans la nation même où l'Assemblée aura son siège temporaire, des fonctionnaires qui soient originaires de ce même pays et en comprennent les mœurs et les usages.

[18°] De plus, pour pouvoir faire face aux dépenses et aux frais indispensables et utiles pour le maintien de la paix, l'exercice du pouvoir judiciaire, la désignation et l'envoi des représentants et des messagers et pour tous les autres besoins, chacun de nous fait promesse et prend engagement de percevoir, par ses propres agents ou en son nom, à l'époque qu'aura fixée l'Assemblée ou sa majorité, la dixième partie des dîmes ainsi que des gains et profits des trois journées, comme déjà dit; puis d'envoyer et faire transporter les fonds sans délai ni retard aux archives publiques, à la disposition du Conseil de l'Assemblée et de ses caissiers. Faute de quoi, le syndic ou le procurateur fiscal de l'Assemblée a le droit et est tenu d'assigner le débiteur devant le Parlement ou Cour pour recouvrer la créance par voie de justice, ainsi que des indemnités, avec intérêts; en outre, il devra prévenir les autres membres et nous inviter — conformément à la foi jurée — à exiger et faire rentrer par une exécution militaire la somme due par le débiteur et ses sujets, indemnités et intérêt compris; ces fonds seront affectés, comme prévu, aux besoins communs de l'Assemblée.

[19°] En outre, arrêtons et voulons que dans ladite Assemblée une voix soit attribuée au roi de France ensemble avec les autres rois et princes de la Gaule, la seconde voix aux rois et princes de la Germanie et la troisième au Doge de Venise ensemble avec les princes et Communes d'Italie. Si le roi de Castille et d'autres rois et princes de la nation hispanique adhéraient à notre alliance, amitié et fraternité, il leur sera semblablement accordé une voix dans notre Assemblée, corps et corporation. Toutefois, si des divergences d'opinions devaient se manifester sur une question entre les délégués des rois et des princes d'une seule et même nation, nous stipulons que le point de vue et le vote de la majorité seront acquis, comme s'ils avaient reçu l'approbation unanime de cette nation; au cas où il y aurait partage égal des suffrages, ce sont les voix des délégués représentant des seigneurs plus haut placés en titres et en mérite qui prévaudront; les autres nations, signataires de notre pacte, choisiront entre les deux parties.

[20°] Pour qu'il ne subsiste aucun doute à cet égard, il est bien stipulé qu'au cas où tel roi ou prince députerait plusieurs délégués dans notre Assemblée, ces délégués ne disposeront à eux tous que d'une seule voix, à savoir celle que possède dans la curie nationale de l'Assemblée celui qui les a envoyés.

[21°] De plus, attendu que l'Ecriture atteste que celui qui aura servi, répandu et défendu la foi du Christ, aura sa place réservée au ciel où les bienheureux jouissent de la vie éternelle, il faut attendre que tous les autres chrétiens voudront de tout leur cœur joindre leurs efforts à une œuvre aussi sainte, aussi pieuse, aussi nécessaire; car celui qui aura refusé de prêter son aide à présent contre les Turcs, manifestera qu'il est de toute évidence l'allié des infidèles et des ennemis de la croix du Christ. C'est pourquoi nous multiplions par l'intermédiaire de nos délégués solennels nos démarches auprès du Souverain Pontife avec tout le zèle et la diligence dont nous sommes capables, en respectant les voies et les formes qu'arrêtera la susdite Assemblée, pour obtenir de Sa Sainteté qu'elle attire l'attention sur le fait que la levée de dîmes est sollicitée en vue de garantir la paix des chrétiens, défendre les fidèles du Christ et combattre les ennemis de la Croix; que le Souverain Pontife, père et pasteur des fidèles, de son auguste clémence et bienveillance, par des bulles authentiques et publiques, accompagnées de sanctions redoutables, concède et confie à des percepteurs par lui nommés et dûment désignés et envoyés, de faire donner, remettre et acquitter les dîmes précitées selon le mode et les conditions qui seront arrêtés par nous et en notre nom; que le Souverain Pontife fasse cesser toutes guerres et dissensions existant entre les princes ecclésiastiques qui sont en dehors de notre traité, et surtout qu'il nous débarrasse de toutes les guerres qui pourraient empêcher de manière ou d'autre de mener à bonne fin la lutte contre les Turcs et de raffermir la paix, ou encore qu'il envoie dans chaque pays un légat qui soit homme de vie exemplaire, probe et expérimenté, muni de pleins pouvoirs, qui connaisse et comprenne la vie, la langue et les usages de ce pays; qu'il déploie zèle et diligence autant qu'il faudra pour que les parties règlent leurs différends à l'amiable. Si toutefois elles s'y refusaient, le légat — en vertu des pouvoirs qu'il aura reçus — terminera et tranchera juridiquement le litige pendant. Enfin que Sa Sainteté réunisse les autres princes et Communes d'Italie pour leur faire remontrance et leur imposer, sous peine de sanctions divines et de châtiments redoutables, d'entreprendre la construction d'une flotte maritime, puisqu'ils sont plus proches voisins des Turcs que les autres peuples; et cela de concert avec les autres chrétiens auxquels ils apporteront leur part proportionnelle de subsides pour l'honneur et la gloire de Dieu ainsi que pour la protection des fidèles, de telle sorte que la grande œuvre de défense de la foi aboutisse au résultat espéré avec d'autant plus d'honneur.

[22°] En outre, pour que la paix ainsi que les précédentes dispositions soient inviolablement observées, nous avons décidé et nous promettons, quand l'un de nous aura été appelé dans la patrie céleste, de ne pas laisser l'un de ses héritiers ou successeurs accéder au pouvoir et entrer en possession d'un royaume, d'une principauté ou d'un domaine aussi longtemps qu'il n'aura pas, avant toute chose, pris l'engagement de respecter avec une fidélité inébranlable l'ensemble des articles précédents ainsi que le suivant et chacun d'eux en particulier, par des lettres patentes avec sceau pendant, comme garantie en commun apportée à chacun de nous.

[23°] Si notre susdite Assemblée ou sa majorité ordonne, décrète ou arrête ultérieurement d'autres mesures, qui semblent propres à contribuer de quelque manière au maintien de la paix et de la justice ainsi qu'à la défense des fidèles du Christ, nous serons attentifs à les appliquer toutes et chacune, efficacement. Nous accomplirons tout ce qu'exige et requiert le lien de la véritable et sincère fraternité; nous exécuterons tout ce qui est inclus dans la présente charte selon la division des matières, et dans la totalité de ses points, clauses, articles, paragraphes et chapitres. En témoignage et confirmation de quoi, chacun de nous, rois et princes, a décidé d'apposer sur les présentes le sceau de sa majesté. Fait et donné, etc.

[Traduit par Konstantin Jelínek, docteur ès lettres].

TRATADO DE PAZ QUE DEBE SER ESTABLECIDA EN TODA LA CRISTIANDAD

A nombre de nuestro Señor Jesucristo. Nosotros, ABC, hacemos del conocimiento de todos y cada uno en particular, para que lo guarden en eterna memoria, que: Al leer los escritos de los historiadores antiguos descubrimos que antaño la cristiandad, copiosa en hombres y riquezas, se encontraba en pleno florecimiento, que fue tal su extensión en latitud y longitud que llegó a abarcar en su seno ciento diez y siete reinos considerables; que dio a luz a tal multitud de hombres que llegó a apoderarse, por largo tiempo, de gran parte de los pueblos paganos, incluso del Santo Sepulcro; y que en aquel entonces no hubo nación en el mundo entero que se atreviese a perturbar el poderío de los cristianos. Mas es bien sabido por todos lo lacerado, destruido y miserable que está hoy en día, despojado de todo su esplendor y magnificencia de otros tiempos. Hace poco, en el seno de la cristiandad misma se operó tal cambio que si alguno de los reyes, príncipes o próceres antiguos resucitase y visitase las tierras cristianas, no reconocería ni siquiera su propio país. Efectivamente, al mismo tiempo que casi el mundo entero encontraba su grandeza en la santidad de la religión cristiana, el astuto Mahoma comenzó por seducir al pequeño pueblo árabe; y al no encontrar resistencia en sus primeras tentativas, no tardó en ganar, poco a poco, tal multitud de gente perdida, que terminó por conquistar las más vastas regiones de África y Asia, conduciéndoles a la más infame traición. Finalmente, los turcos villanos, quienes en estos últimos tiempos sometieron a su dominación al glorioso Imperio griego y tras él a un gran número de provincias y reinos cristianos, arrebataron una cantidad casi infinita de almas de las regiones cristianas, llevándose todo en calidad de botín, demoliendo o reduciendo a ruinas múltiples monasterios y magníficos templos de Dios; asimismo cometieron y perpetraron un sinnúmero de atrocidades.
¡ Ay, áurea tierra! Ay, cristiandad, ornato de las naciones, ¿cómo se ha desvanecido toda tu gloria, cómo has perdido tus más bellos colores? ¿Dónde está aquel hermoso de tus hombres? ¿Dónde la veneración que te tributaban todos los pueblos, dónde tu majestad real, dónde, la gloria? ¿De qué te han servido tantas victorias si tan pronto debías figurar, vencida, entre cortejo triunfal? ¿De qué sirve que hayas resistido el poderío de los jefes paganos si ahora te faltan fuerzas para afrontar las acometidas de tus vecinos? ¡ Ay, fortuna! ¡ Ay, vicisitudes del destino! ¡Cuán efímeros son los imperios, cuán mutables los reinos, cuán frágiles los gobiernos! No es fácil discernir la causa de tal cambio y de tal ruina,

porque los designios de Dios son impenetrables. Como en otros tiempos, los campos no son menos
fértiles que antes, ni menos fecundos los rebaños, ni menos prósperos los viñedos, ni menos lucrativas
las minas de plata y de oro; los hombres son sensatos, industriosos, valientes, expertos en cosas múlti-
ples, las bellas letras florecen como nunca. Entonces, ¿ qué es lo que ha humillado tanto al cristianismo,
que de los ciento diez y siete reinos anteriormente mencionados, no más de diez y seis han subsistido en
el seno de la cristiandad? ¿ Acaso serán los innumerables pecados que Dios quiere castigar, como antaño
lo hizo más de una vez, según vemos en el Viejo Testamento? Nos parece, por lo tanto, que es preciso
considerar con atención ese estado de cosas con el fin de rectificar cuanto sea impío y de apaciguar,
por medio de actos de contrición, a la Majestad Divina, evidentemente ofendida a causa de alguna
iniquidad. Empero, ya que nosotros sabemos que Dios trata justa y misericordiosamente a quienes
castiga en este mundo, que él mismo tiene a los hombres por sus hijos y que corrige y reprende a los
que ama, induciéndoles por los largos caminos de la adversidad a actos de virtud, por ello ponemos
nuestras esperanzas en el Señor y en su justa causa, teniendo por seguro que no podemos realizar nada
más conveniente a nuestra piedad, nada más congruente con nuestra probidad y nada más digno de
nuestra gloria, que hacer todo lo que esté a nuestro alcance para establecer entre los cristianos una
paz verdadera, pura y duradera, así como unidad y caridad, y para que la fe de Cristo sea defendida
frente al turco feroz. Porque, con este fin nos han sido confiados los reinos y principados, para que
celebremos la paz con todo el afán y diligencia posibles, para que la posición de la cristiandad sea man-
tenida, las guerras contra los infieles llevadas hasta su feliz término y el territorio de la cristian-
dad protegido y ensanchado. A este fin deben y tienen que emplear sus esfuerzos todos los hombres,
todas las naciones, todos los reyes y príncipes, con ánimo jubiloso y resuelto. Ya que nos llamamos
cristianos, debemos velar por que sea protegida la religión cristiana; y si no queremos levantarnos
contra Cristo, estamos obligados a batirnos por su fe y mantenernos a su lado. Porque el Espíritu
Santo condena a los que no sostienen lucha junto con él, que no se levantan en defensa de los puntos
flojos y no se colocan como un muro ante la casa del Israel. Ni la dulzura del país natal, ni los palacios
magníficos, ni la abundancia de riquezas deben apartar a nadie del servicio a Dios. Es preciso
servirle al que por nosotros no temió sufrir la muerte en la cruz, que premiará a todo fiel con el don
de la patria celeste, nuestra verdadera patria, donde hay moradas inmensas, riquezas incomparables
y vida eterna. Así, por muy lamentable que sea actualmente la suerte de los griegos y pese a nuestra
aflicción por el desastre de Constantinopla y de otros países, nosotros, ávidos de la gloria, había-
mos de desear la ocasión que nos permita reservarnos el honor de ser llamados defensores y salva-
dores del nombre cristiano. Por eso, deseando poner fin a las guerras, pillaje, turbulencias, incendios
y masacres, infortunios que — según ya hemos referido con profundo dolor — han cercado la cristian-
dad misma casi por todos lados devastando los campos, destruyendo las ciudades, lacerando las
tierras y abrumando, por desgracias incontables, reinos y principados, deseosos, pues, de que cesen y
queden extirpados todos estos males, de que se arribe, por unidad laudable, al estado conveniente
de caridad y fraternidad mutua, con conocimiento de causa y al cabo de una deliberación madu-
ra, habiendo implorado sobre nuestro proyecto la gracia del Espíritu Santo y consultado y obte-
nido la aprobación de nuestros prelados, príncipes, próceres, nobles y doctores en derecho divino y
humano, — hemos resuelto concluir, en la forma siguiente, un pacto entablando unidad, paz, frater-

nidad y concordia inflexibles, por la veneración de Dios y preservación de la fe por siempre jamás, por nosotros y por nuestros herederos y sucesores venideros.

[1]   En primer lugar, sobre el honor de la fe católica y sobre nuestra palabra de rey y príncipe declaramos y prometemos, a partir de esta hora y de este día mostrar y observar unos frente a otros fraternidad pura, verdadera y sincera, no recurrir a armas unos contra otros, cualquiera que fuere la naturaleza de nuestras disenciones, diferencias y agravios, y no permitir a nadie hacerlo a nuestro nombre; más bien, conforme al texto y sentido de lo dispuesto en los artículos que siguen a continuación, prometemos respaldar el uno al otro frente a toda persona viviente que pretendiere invadir hostilmente a nosotros o a uno de nosotros de hecho y sin edicto legítimo.

[2]   En segundo lugar, prometemos que ninguno de nosotros prestará ayuda o consejo ni conspirará contra la persona del otro y que ni nosotros por sí mismo ni por medio de otro u otros pondremos en peligro la seguridad o la vida de su persona, ni nos asociaremos con aquéllos que quieran complotar contra ella, sino que, al contrario, velaremos por la preservación de su salud, su vida y su honor, según nuestras posibilidades.

[3]   En tercer lugar, garantizamos en la forma antes dicha, que si uno o varios de los súbditos de alguno de nosotros perpetrare o perpetraren devastaciones, pillaje, rapiña, incendios o cualquier otro tipo de crímenes en los reinos, principados o dominios de uno de nos-otros, no será violada o rota dicha paz y unidad, sino que los infractores serán obligados a reparar los daños; si se muestra imposible obtener la satisfacción a las buenas, serán citados ante la justicia por aquél dentro de cuya jurisdicción residan los delincuentes o se constate el crimen, de modo que los daños ocasionados sean reparados a expensas de los culpables y éstos, debidamente castigados, según la naturaleza del delito perpetrado. Si los malhechores se niegan de aparecer ante el juicio, su señor, cualquiera que sea, competente ora en virtud del domicilio ora según el lugar del delito y sin que el uno espere al otro, deberá y tendrá que perseguir e impugnarlos. Si uno de nosotros, dentro de cuya jurisdicción resida el delincuente o en cuyo territorio haya sido perpetrado el delito y detenido el infractor, omitiere o vacilare en aplicar las disposiciones antes dichas, será objeto de la misma sanción que la infligida al culpable. La parte ofendida o perjudi-cada tendrá el derecho de perseguir y citar ante la justicia a ése de nosotros ante el Par-lamento o Consistorio previsto más adelante.

[4] En cuarto lugar determinamos: si alguno o algunos de los no adheridos a nuestra convención, caridad y fraternidad, lanzare o intentare lanzar la guerra contra cualquiera de nosotros sin perjuicio o provocación de nuestra parte — cosa que, a nuestro parecer, no hay que temer mientras subsista dicha amistad y caridad — nuestra Congregación prevista más adelante, actuando a nombre de todos los signatarios de este tratado y aún cuando el nuestro socio agredido no lo pidiere, enviará sin demora, a expensas comunes, su delegación solemne, la que se trasladará — con el fin de zanjar la disputa y concertar la paz — a un lugar conveniente a ambas partes donde, en presencia de las partes en litigio o de sus representantes investidos de plenos poderes, con todo empeño y diligencia pretenderán restablecer la concordia y la paz entre los adversarios, por vía amistosa, si es posible; si no, impeliéndoles a elegir árbitros o a reclamar sus derechos ante el juez competente o ante el Parlamento o Consistorio previsto más adelante. Si a causa o por culpa de la parte que inició la guerra resultare imposible restablecer la paz y la unidad por uno de los medios citados, todos nosotros sin excepción, por decisión unánime y tomada en perfecto acuerdo, acudiremos en ayuda de nuestro socio oprimido o que se estare defendiendo, contribuyendo a su defensa con los diezmos provenientes de nuestros reinos, así como con las utilidades y beneficios calculados sobre el promedio anual de dichos medios empleados por nuestros súbditos en el mantenimiento de sus casas y menajes durante tres días cada año. La suma y la duración de estas exacciones serán consideradas y fijadas por nuestra Congregación o por su mayoría según se estime apropiado y conveniente respecto a la consecución de la paz por nuestro socio atacado.

[5] Con miras a una eliminación todavía más acertada de las disenciones y guerras, ya que sólo el pensar en ellas engendra sufrimiento en los que se las infligen mutuamente, y a fin de robustecer la paz también entre los demás fieles de Jesucristo que no forman parte de este tratado, estipulamos y dictamos que, en caso de que surgieren discordias o guerra entre otros príncipes o magnates cristianos no incorporados a nuestra fraternidad, nuestra Congregación mencionada más adelante enviará, en nuestro nombre y a nuestras expensas comunes, una delegación, pretendiendo restablecer la concordia entre los adversarios, valiéndose de un procedimiento amistoso, si es posible, o por la vía de la justicia, según se ha estipulado; si ambas partes — o una de ellas — no quisieren aceptar el acuerdo y desistir de la guerra y de las luchas, el que hubiere iniciado la guerra o que se resistiere a cesarla será obligado a ello por los medios y bajo las formas determinadas en el artículo precedente.

[6] Asimismo estipulamos que los que se atrevieren en cualquier forma a violar nuestra presente paz bajo cualquier pretexto no deberán ni podrán ser recibidos, empleados,

protegidos o auxiliados, ni concedidos de favor alguno en ninguno de nuestros reinos, principados, dominios, territorios o distritos, castillos, ciudades, pueblos o fortalezas, antes bien, sin tener en cuenta cualquier salvoconducto serán arrestados, capturados y castigados como violadores de la paz general, correspondiendo la sanción a la naturaleza del crimen o delito perpetrado.

[7] Además, disponemos y ordenamos por las presentes a todos nuestros funcionarios y súbditos y a cada uno en particular no prestar ayuda y protección a nadie — tanto en común como en particular — y no conceder ni proporcionar a nadie un salvoconducto, general o especial, sin establecer previamente la condición particular y explícita de que dicho salvoconducto o protección no precaverán a la persona a la que han sido otorgados, de las medidas que se tomen a fin de proteger y defender nuestra presente paz, sino que, contra el que fuere inculpado, sospechado o acusado de haber infringido la paz, se podrá proceder — sin que nadie se oponga a ello — por los medios de justicia antes mencionados.

[8] El que se asociare conscientemente con el violador de la presente paz y le prestare, bajo cualquier pretexto, apoyo, ayuda o favor, que recibiere, protegiere o defendiere al mismo o se atreviere a proporcionarle un salvoconducto contra nuestra union, será reprimido con el mismo castigo como el reo.

[9] Considerando que no puede haber mantenimiento afectuoso de la paz sin justicia, ni justicia sin paz, que esta última nace de la justicia y en ella se preserva, que nosotros y nuestros súbditos no podríamos vivir en paz sin la justicia, asociamos por ello la justicia con la causa de la paz. Empero, la ley del orden judicial ha sufrido múltiples transformaciones en el transcurso del tiempo hasta degenerar, paulatinamente, por completo, de manera que la práctica por intepretación le ha dado un aspecto completamente diferente; por lo que, contemplando la confusión absoluta en la que han caído dichos reglamentos, estimamos indispensable hacer surgir del seno de la naturaleza un derecho nuevo, teniendo en cuenta los hábitos, costumbres y usanzas propios de nuestra época y de nuestras diferentes tierras, reinos y principados, así como adoptar nuevos remedios para hacer frente a los nuevos abusos, que permitan recompensar a las personas virtuosas y aplastar a las viciosas con los martillos de los castigos. Para sujetarnos a un determinado orden al tratar los diferentes puntos prevemos, primero, un Consistorio General que se reunirá,

a nombre de todos nosotros y de nuestra Congregación, en el lugar donde ésta tenga su sede temporal. De dicho Consistorio, como de una fuente, manarán arroyos de justicia hacia todos lados. Este tribunal estará organizado, según el número y rango de sus miembros, así como según los estatutos que le rijan, con arreglo a lo que concluya y decida nuestra Congregación o su mayoría.

[10] A fin de que los litigios suscitados ante este tribunal sean llevados a su término, sin demoras interminables, estimamos que el juez mismo y sus asesores procederán y harán justicia a los litigantes conforme a la naturaleza del pleito, en forma simple y clara, sin figura ni estrépito judicial y proscribiendo todo subterfugio y dilación frustratoria.

[11] También estipulamos que en caso de que surgieren nuevas disputas y discordias entre nosotros, reyes, príncipes y demás signatarios de este tratado, uno respecto a otro deba y esté obligado a comparecer y litigar, conforme a la ley, ante nuestro tribunal mencionado, observando los estatutos, decretos y reglamentos dictados y decretados por nuestros delegados y representantes o por la mayoría de la Congregación, según se ha dicho.

[12] Asimismo, resolvemos que nuestra Congregación tenga la libre y plena facultad de admitir a nuestra presente paz, unidad, caridad y fraternidad a todos los reyes, príncipes y magnates cristianos hasta el momento no incorporados a nuestra unión; de aceptar compromisos recíprocos — por medio de cartas expedidas y aceptadas por ambas partes — actuando en nuestro nombre, como si nosotros mismos lo hiciéramos, entendiéndose que después de consumada la adhesión, la misma Congregación nos informará sin demora al efecto, para que nosotros podamos y estemos en condiciones de recibir a los nuevos socios con toda la afección fraternal, como es debido.

[13] Considerando que esta unión, entendimiento y caridad hayan sido concluidos y constituidos principalmente para la gloria y el honor de la Majestad Divina, de la Santa Iglesia Romana y de la fe católica, así como para que sea posible prestar la ayuda más eficaz posible a los fieles de Cristo que sufren bajo la férula del príncipe de los turcos, enemigo más encarnizado del nombre cristiano, por ello nosotros, reyes y príncipes — llamando como testigo a nuestro Señor Jesucristo, a Santa María, su gloriosísima Madre, y a la Santa Iglesia

Romana — prometemos defender y proteger a la religión cristiana y a todos los fieles oprimidos por el príncipe abominable de los turcos, mancomunando nuestras fuerzas y recursos, declarados y fijados en forma proporcional; para adquirir y reunir éstos daremos y entregaremos, mientras sea necesario, todos los diezmos percibidos en nuestros reinos, principados y dominios en beneficio de las iglesias y de los eclesiásticos y los religiosos, agregando a ellos nuestros precitados provechos y beneficios, así como los de nuestros súbditos, que representen los gastos de tres días al año, según se ha determinado. No dejaremos de perseguir al enemigo, si nuestra Congregación lo considera oportuno, mientras no sea expulsado de las tierras cristianas o hasta que no sea decidido unánimemente concertar la paz, la que no será concluida a menos que se estime que por medio de la misma quedará garantizada la seguridad de los cristianos circundantes.

[14] Además, ya que es preciso prevenirlo todo con habilidad, precaución y diligencia, para que no terminen por caer en desgracia los imprudentes, decidimos que sea fijado, por una resolución conjunta de nuestra Congregación unánime o de su mayoría, el momento oportuno para lanzar el ataque contra el enemigo, las fuerzas terrestres y navales para llevar la guerra, a qué generales confiar el mando, qué máquinas y medios de guerra emplear, así como el lugar de reunión de todas las fuerzas terrestres para marchar contra los turcos. Del mismo modo, la forma de procurar víveres a precios justos, así como alojamiento en ciudades, aldeas y otros lugares oportunos. También, las medidas a tomar para introducir una moneda única en el ejército, con el fin de salvar dificultades a los soldados mientras estén en marcha, en guarnición o durante su retorno. Además, decídase en común, a quién atribuir el territorio que se logre arrancar de manos o del poder de los enemigos, según se reconozca y juzgue más benéfico a los intereses de la religión cristiana y a la seguridad futura de los fieles, para evitar que el enemigo, estimulado por la negligencia o incapacidad de los posesores, no inflija a los fieles daños mayores.

[15] Igualmente estipulamos que — después de concluido nuestro pacto — cada uno de nosotros proceda sin tardanza a la exacción de los subsidios, según se ha previsto, en su respectivo reino, principado o dominio, dentro de las formas y reglas que dicte al efecto la misma Congregación o su mayoría de manera que la tarea divina sea ejecutada sin demora y los fieles de Cristo socorridos.

[16] También, para que sea debidamente cumplido, en general y en particular, cuanto precede y sigue, cada uno de nosotros nos comprometemos y prometemos, en la forma supra-

dicha, enviar el domingo de *Reminiscere* más próximo del año mil cuatro cientos sesenta y cuatro después del nacimiento del Señor, a la ciudad de Basilea, en Alemania, a sus representantes escogidos de entre hombres de relieve y de gran valor, investidos de los más amplios poderes y de su sigilo. Éstos estarán en sesión en dicho lugar durante los cinco años siguientes y formarán, constituirán y representarán a nombre nuestro, así como a nombre de todos los demás miembros y de los que lleguen a serlo, un cuerpo, comunidad y corporación verdadera. Expirado el quinquenio de la Congregación de Basilea, la misma Congregación se celebrará, durante un segundo quinquenio, en la ciudad de N, en Francia, y durante el tercer quinquenio, en la ciudad de N, en Italia, rigiéndose por las reglas y cláusulas estimadas como prudentes y aplicadas previamente a Basilea; de modo que la Congregación cambiará de sede de un quinquenio a otro realizando un circuito, hasta el día en que la Congregación misma o la mayoría de sus miembros convenga en disponer y adoptar otros reglamentos. La Congregación tendrá un solo Consejo, propio y especial, con un Presidente, N., que será su padre y cabeza, mientras que nosotros, los demás reyes y príncipes de la cristiandad, seremos sus miembros. Sobre todos nosotros y nuestros súbditos, así como sobre los que sean admitidos posteriormente, dicha corporación ejercerá la jurisdicción voluntaria y la contenciosa, junto con los imperios mero y mixto, según las disposiciones que dicte y fije la misma Congregación o su mayoría. Finalmente, la misma tendrá su propio emblema, su sigilo, su tesoro común y su archivo público, su síndico, su procurador fiscal, sus funcionarios, así como todos los demás derechos atribuidos y pertenecientes, en cualquier forma, a una corporación lícita y justa.

[17]   A fin de que se conserven intactos los derechos de cada país resolvemos que sean designados en la Congregación a los cargos superiores en la nación donde ésta tenga su sede temporal personas provenientes de esa nación que conozcan y comprendan sus costumbres y usanzas.

[18]   Además, para poder cubrir las expensas y los gastos útiles e indispensables para el mantenimiento de la paz, el ejercicio del poder judicial, la designación y el envío de representantes y mensajeros, y para todas las demás necesidades, cada uno de nosotros se compromete y promete percibir, por medio de sus agentes o en su nombre, en el tiempo que fije la Congregación o la mayoría de sus miembros, la décima parte de los diezmos, así como de los beneficios y provechos de los tres días mencionados; luego, transferir dichos fondos inmediatamente al archivo público a la orden del Consejo de la Congregación y de sus recaudadores. Y si omitiere hacerlo, el síndico o el procurador fiscal de la Congre-

gación tendrá el derecho y el deber de citar al deudor ante el Parlamento o el Tribunal para reivindicar por la vía judicial el dinero así como la indemnización con intereses. Además, deberá prevenir a los demás miembros y exhortarles — remitiéndose a la fe jurada — a adquirir por medio de una expedición militar la suma pendiente incluyendo la indemnización y los intereses; estos fondos serán empleados, según se ha previsto, para hacer frente a las necesidades comunes de la Congregación.

[19] Además, resolvemos y queremos que en dicha Congregación sea atribuida una voz al rey de Francia conjuntamente con los demás reyes y príncipes de Galia, la segunda voz a los reyes y príncipes de Germania, y la tercera voz al dux de Venecia junto con los príncipes y las Comunidades de Italia. Si el rey de Castilla u otros reyes y príncipes de la nación hispánica se adhirieren a nuestra unión, amistad y fraternidad, les será concedida análogamente una voz en la Congregación, cuerpo y corporación. Si surgieren y se manifestaren opiniones contrarias relativas a un determinado asunto entre los delegados de los reyes y de los príncipes de una misma nación, estipulamos que sea el punto de vista y el voto de la mayoría que tendrá la misma validez como si hubiera recibido la aprobación unánime de esa nación; en caso de empate se reconocerá la prevalencia de los delegados representantes de los señores más distinguidos por sus méritos y rango. Y si fueren iguales en méritos y rango, a las demás naciones adheridas a este pacto les competerá optar por una de las dos partes.

[20] Para que no subsista duda ninguna al respecto se establece que, en caso de que alguno de nuestros reyes o príncipes envíe varios delegados a dicha Congregación, todos esos delegados contarán con una sola voz, a saber, la que corresponde al propio diputador en su respectiva curia nacional de la Congregación.

[21] Además — considerando que la Sagrada Escritura atestigua que le está reservado un lugar en el cielo, donde todos los bienaventurados gozan de la vida eterna, al que ayude, aumente o defienda la fe de Cristo — es de esperar que todos los demás cristianos coadyuven animosos una causa tan santa, tan pía y tan necesaria, porque el que en estos días se niegue a prestar ayuda contra los turcos se declarará aliado patente de los infieles y enemigos de la cruz de Cristo. Por ello acordamos que todos nosotros, por mediación de nuestros delegados solemnes, nos dirijamos al Soberano Pontífice, desplegando todos los esfuerzos y diligencia y observando los medios y formas que determine la Congregación

precitada, para conseguir que Su Santidad enfoque su atención sobre el hecho de que las percepciones de diezmos se solicitan con miras a garantizar la paz de los cristianos, a defender a los fieles de Cristo y a combatir a los enemigos de la Cruz; que el Soberano Pontífice, padre y pastor de los fieles, de su benigna clemencia, por bulas públicas y auténticas, previendo sanciones severas, conceda y ordene a los perceptores por él nombrados y debidamente designados y enviados, cuidar de que sean entregados, remitidos y solventados los diezmos precitados, bajo las formas y condiciones que le sean ofrecidas por nosotros y a nuestro nombre; que el Soberano Pontífice haga cesar todas las guerras y disenciones entre los príncipes eclesiásticos no adheridos a nuestro tratado, principalmente a las guerras que pudieren obstaculizar, de una manera u otra, que sea llevada a su feliz término la guerra contra los turcos y preservada la paz mencionada; o bien que envía a cada país a un legato, hombre de vida impecable, probado y experimentado, investido de plenos poderes al efecto, que conozca y comprenda el modo de vivir, el idioma y las costumbres de ese país, y quien empleará los esfuerzos y la diligencia adecuados para que las partes resuelvan sus disputas por vía amistosa. Si éstas, empero, se negaren a hacerlo, el legato — en virtud de los poderes que le han sido conferidos — terminará y decidirá judicialmente el litigio pendiente. Y, finalmente, que Su Santidad convoque a los demás príncipes y Comunidades de Italia con el fin de amonestar y pedirles, so pena de la sanción divina y de castigos severos, que ellos, como vecinos más cercanos de los turcos que las otras naciones, emprendan la construcción de una flota marítima, obrando en cooperación con los demás cristianos a los que aportarán su parte proporcional de subsidios para la gloria y el honor de Dios, así como para proteger a los fieles, de manera que la gran obra de la defensa de la fe alcance los resultados anhelados con honores mayores todavía.

[22] Además, para que sea observada de un modo inviolable la paz, así como las disposiciones precedentes, hemos resuelto y prometemos que, cuando uno de nosotros sea llamado a la patria celeste, no permitiremos a ningún heredero o sucesor tomar posesión del poder del reino, principado o dominio, sin que antes se comprometa a observar con fidelidad inflexible todo lo supra e infrascrito, en general así como en particular, por medio de sus letras patentes con sigilo pendiente, dadas como garantía común a nuestra Congregación, a la disposición de cualquiera de nosotros.

[23] Si nuestra Congregación o su mayoría ordena, decreta y dicta posteriormente otras medidas, que se vean apropiadas y conducentes de alguna manera al mantenimiento de la paz y de la justicia, así como a la defensa de los cristianos fieles, las observaremos y

aplicaremos eficazmente, en su conjunto y en particular. Ejecutaremos lo que exige y requiere el vínculo de la verdadera y sincera fraternidad y que está incluido en nuestras presentes letras, según sus diferentes asuntos, y en la totalidad de sus puntos, cláusulas, artículos, sentencias y capítulos.

En cuyo testimonio y confirmación cada uno de nosotros, reyes y príncipes, ha decidido añadir a la presente el sigilo de su majestad. Hecho y dado, etc.

[*Traducido por Eva Šimková*]